VICTORIAN FURNITURE

WITH PRICES

DAVID P. LINDQUIST
AND CAROLINE C. WARREN

Wallace-Homestead Book Company
Radnor, Pennsylvania

Copyright © 1995 by David P. Lindquist and Caroline C. Warren
All Rights Reserved

Published in Radnor, Pennsylvania 19089, by Wallace-Homestead,
a division of Chilton Book Company

Designed by Anthony Jacobson
Manufactured in the United States of America

Library of Congress Cataloging in Publication Data
Lindquist, David P.
    Victorian furniture with prices / David P. Lindquist and Caroline
C. Warren.
        p.   cm.
    Includes bibliographical references and index.
    ISBN 0-87069-664-5 (pbk.)
    1. Furniture, Victorian—Collectors and collecting—Catalogs.
2. Furniture—Styles.   I. Warren, Caroline C.   II. Title.
NK2390.L56   1995
749.213'09'034075—dc20   95-10554
                                                              CIP

1 2 3 4 5 6 7 8 9 0   3 2 1 0 9 8 7 6 5 4

To Maggie and Chris
and all the staff at
Whitehall at the Villa

———————

CONTENTS

ACKNOWLEDGMENTS

It would be impossible to do a book of this scope without the help of many people. Dealers specializing in Victorian furniture generously shared their expertise with us, loaned us photographs, and allowed us to photograph their inventories. Owners of fabulous private collections graciously allowed us into their homes to photograph their Victorian furniture. Auction houses around the country loaned us photographs from their auction catalogs. We were also fortunate to be able to use the research collections at several fine libraries. We would like to thank the following people for their generous support and help: Brian Witherell; Joan Bogart; Larry Kemper; Priscilla St. Germain; Jim Butt; Lee Lynch; James Creech; Jack and Pat Rudiger; Mr. and Mrs. Joseph K. Spiers, Mrs. J. C. Powell and Miss Mary Collins Powell of Tarboro, North Carolina; Bill Turner; the City of Durham Parks and Recreation Department and the Friends of West Point, Inc.; Margaret Pless; Lauri Clay at Neal Auction Company; Cindy Edwards at Edwards Antiques in Pittsboro, North Carolina; Peter N. Tocci and Ricky M. Dixon, R. G. Lassiter House, Oxford, North Carolina; Joe Howard of Apex, North Carolina; Carl Voncannon of the Furniture Library in High Point, North Carolina; Rachel Frew of the Sloan Art Library at the University of North Carolina at Chapel Hill; the reference librarians at Winterthur Library, Wilmington, Delaware.

Finally, we would like to thank our editor at Chilton, Kathy Conover, for her encouragement and patience. And most of all, we would like to thank the staff at Whitehall at the Villa for their ongoing support.

Introduction

As you look through this book, you will be astounded by the great variety of styles that can all be called *Victorian.* The Victorian market truly offers something for everyone, with a huge range of prices and styles to suit almost every taste. This era takes its name from Queen Victoria, the English monarch who reigned from 1837 to 1901. Our book covers Victorian furniture in America from about 1830 to 1900, a period of immense energy and optimism during which furniture in exuberant designs was produced.

Each chapter in the book is devoted to a type of Victorian furniture: Gothic Revival, cottage, Rococo Revival, Renaissance Revival, patent, Eastlake, and golden oak. While these all constitute distinct styles, there are some underlying characteristics that apply overall. There was a love of rich effect, manifested in pieces of massive size and in the use of high-relief carving, flame veneers, burl panels, line-incised decoration, gilt or ebonized accents, marquetry, porcelain plaques, marble, tufted upholstery and rich fabrics. Even towards the end of the century, when reform was attempted in the name of Eastlake and the English Aesthetic Movement, American mass-produced versions still could not resist ornamentation. Victorians are famous for their "horror vacuii": no surface could be left without decoration. This holds true for furniture throughout the entire period—even on many pieces dating from the reform-influenced 1870s and 1880s.

Picturesque Eclecticism

A good way to understand what seemed beautiful to the Victorians is found in the idea of picturesque eclecticism.[1] We can better understand Victorian aesthetics by realizing that it was fundamentally Romantic, very different from 18th-century classicism and also from 20th-century modernism, two sensibilities that currently appeal to us. Ideas about the picturesque were germinated by the 18th-century author Edmund Burke, who wrote *A Philosophical Enquiry into the Origin of Our Ideas of the Sublime and Beautiful* (1757). Burke explored the emotions associated with the sublime and beautiful, and he found that astonishment and terror heightened the experience of beautiful things. These qualities were celebrated in Romantic art, and the earliest phase of Victorian furniture, the Gothic

---

1. A concept originating with Carroll L. V. Meeks in his work *The Railroad Station* (New Haven: Yale University Press, 1956).

Revival, is rooted in these notions about the picturesque.

For the Victorians, the picturesque translated into aesthetic pleasure found in visual surprises, which took the form of unexpected silhouettes or shapes, variety in texture and decorative treatment, and sharp contrasts. Victorian furniture often displays a virtual cacophony of unusual shapes and motifs with little overall unity. We might be tempted to look at these creations and think the designers had aimed for unity and failed. They had not. The kind of tension created by jarring elements is exactly what appealed to the Victorian sensibility. They wanted every inch to be interesting—by virtue of its shape, texture or decoration—rather than have the piece as a whole embody the classical ideals of good proportion and unity of design.

In contrast to the Victorian aesthetic, 18th-century classicism valued an overall unity, which was achieved through fine proportional relationships between parts to the whole, often accomplished through repetition of a single small decorative motif. The Victorians could never limit themselves to repetition of a single decorative element. They insisted on variety and contrast. The whole idea that parts should make up a coherent, unified whole—and the classical means to achieve it—was rejected by Victorian furniture makers.

Victorian aesthetics also rejected the principle that designs should be primarily functional. With our 20th-century viewpoint, most of us look at Victorian furniture and find it impractical. For Victorians, form did not follow function. The Victorian love of the picturesque meant that visual qualities were paramount, with concerns about function lagging far behind. In Victorian furniture, dramatic forms were valued for their visual impact, even though they might be structurally weak. Victorian high-backed chairs, seating furniture with scrolling and curved backs and tables with central pedestal supports make interesting visual statements, but at a sacrifice to structural integrity.

A significant function of Victorian furniture was to convey the status and importance of the owner. This was achieved through rich effect and also through sheer bulk. Furniture of great size and weight created a grand and formal look and reflected on the owner's station in life. The honorific function of Victorian furniture comes across clearly in the massive sideboards, ten-foot hall stands, eight-foot bedsteads and dressers, and all sorts of weighty pieces.

What about the other half of "picturesque eclecticism"? The idea of eclecticism is seen in the many varied styles used as inspiration for Victorian furniture. Furniture designers studied the masters' works and the old historical styles, but not for the sake of copying them. The idea was to create a new synthesis from those styles. The Victorians were far less interested in reproduction than in originality. Over the course of the 19th century, designers borrowed freely from the Middle Ages, the Renaissance, the Baroque, the Rococo style of 18th-century France, Japanese decorative arts, and even exotic Moorish designs. They did not feel constrained by notions of academic correctness (some might say good taste), but mined earlier styles purely to suit their whimsy. In this great age of empire building, styles were appropriated worldwide. So although we can divide the era into several distinct periods, there are many pieces that display features of more than one style.

It has been said that Victorian furniture represents the first truly American style in furniture. While it is true that Victorian furniture did not *copy* historical styles, the inspiration was certainly European in design, coming from imported furniture and European style books, and—this is important—often brought into American culture by recent European immigrants, especially those who fled

France and Germany after the revolutions of the 1840s. The influence of French- and German-born immigrant cabinetmakers, carvers and designers cannot be underestimated in American Victorian furniture. They were major players in the 19th-century American furniture industry.

Technological Innovation

The originality and variety prized in furniture and the decorative arts correspond to the love of progress that epitomized Victorian culture. This was a time of tremendous technological innovation, and each new mechanical invention was greeted with pride. Technology and the capability of machines were allowed to drive design to a great extent—so much so that reform was attempted during the last quarter century in response to the shoddy design on display at the great midcentury international exhibitions. But we should note that although the reformers were very much in earnest, their reforms were embraced by only a few, and otherwise their ideas were watered down almost beyond recognition by the time they reached the broad population. Most people still loved every bit of Victorian ornamentation, despite the reformers. Socialites in Manhattan might be impressed by the clean, spare lines of true Eastlake furniture, but settlers on the prairie wanted all the ornament that new factories could produce.

Quality Levels and Pricing

How does the market set a value on Victorian furniture? Several factors come into play—including quality of design, workmanship, a known maker, condition, rarity, provenance, and usefulness for today's lifestyle. The work of several fine cabinetmaking firms is known for good design and workmanship, and thus highly valued. For example, makers like Belter and Herter Brothers are currently expensive. However, poor condition, even for these makers, will lower the price. A piece by an unknown maker in poor condition should be shunned or bought only at bargain prices. An especially rare form can command a higher price. Knowing who owned the piece—perhaps one of the great robber barons or railroad magnates of the 19th century—can add to the value. The one aspect that can be particularly problematic with Victorian furniture is how useful a piece will be for today's lifestyle.

The real problem in the marketplace for Victorian furniture is not poor design or craftsmanship but size. Many pieces are simply not practical in today's homes. Towering hallstands and massive beds just don't fit into most houses. Consequently, the market is not as strong for such things.

Serious scholarship on Victorian furniture is still relatively new and is just beginning to piece together a picture of the 19th-century furniture trade. The old stereotype of cheap, mass-produced Victorian furniture made of shoddy materials is being reexamined as furniture historians begin to document many of the smaller cabinetmaking firms that produced extraordinary pieces. There was, of course, a great deal of factory-produced furniture, made to suit a range of pocketbooks. However, in recent years, the market has been exciting for the work of the fine cabinetmaking firms of John Henry Belter, Herter Brothers, J. and J. W. Meeks, Alexander Roux, Kimbel and Cabus, and others. Not surprisingly, just as there is a clear difference in quality between the production of smaller firms and mechanized factories, there is a huge difference in prices. Those pieces by known makers have been showing up in prestigious auctions with increasing regularity since the early 1980s.

In the last 20 years important books have been published and exhibitions mounted on Victorian styles and makers. Books and corresponding museum exhibitions of Gothic Revival, John Henry Belter, Herter Brothers, Eastlake, and the Aesthetic Movement have provided us with information on fine makers and interesting design movements. This kind of scholarship almost always enhances the value of the subject being studied. The trend is certainly towards more scholarship on 19th-century furniture and more interest in building serious collections. As 18th-century American furniture becomes increasingly scarce and prohibitively expensive, we are seeing more serious collectors of American Victorian furniture.

Museum collecting has also changed radically in the last ten years or so. Regional museums cannot compete for 18th-century goods. The finest examples are often already in museums. To build exciting, affordable collections, museums have turned to 19th-century pieces for which a $50,000 expenditure buys quality and rarity that would perhaps cost $500,000 to over $1,000,000 for a comparable 18th-century item. Also, museums of the South, Midwest and West have realized that local history is more strongly grounded in the 19th century than the 18th—another very good reason to collect 19th-century pieces.

Victorian furniture has become so important in some areas of the market that an "upper tier" of dealers has emerged—just as existed for years in the period American, English and French markets. These dealers often ask two or three times what a piece would bring at auction or from a generalist. They try to deal only in the most exemplary, labeled or attributed pieces in the finest original state. In dealing and collecting at a rarefied level, subtle distinctions—and the prestige of the dealer—become highly important to value.

A number of these high-end pieces are featured in this book. We have benefitted from the help of several dealers in fine Victorian furniture. Picture captions will sometimes include the notation "dealer estimate." This refers to price ranges provided by such a specialized dealer, and we defer to their expertise at this level of the market. Buying from a specialist means that you do not have to scour the countryside seeking the perfect piece; they will do the work for you and will bring you the highest quality. They will, of course, charge accordingly. The prices of a specialist tell us the value of a piece at its highest level, but that does not rule out the possibility that you might find a similar piece at a lower level of the market. It is worth remembering that since Victorian furniture is still not universally appreciated, one can (with luck) buy a fine piece by a known maker for less money at auction or through a general dealer. Collectors of Victorian furniture can still "hit the jackpot" at estate sales, auctions, and general antiques shops, partly because some dealers still don't realize that there is a difference between factory Victorian and fine Victorian. As we say in the antiques business, knowledge pays.

Aside from this rather glamorous segment of the Victorian market, there is factory-made Victorian furniture at every antiques mall and small antiques shop in America. This kind of furniture is plentiful, so you have the opportunity to pick and choose carefully. With so much available, you must insist on good condition, solid construction, and pleasing design. There is no need to buy a piece in poor condition since you will undoubtedly find another in good shape. With this in mind, all of the prices in our book refer to pieces in *good* condition. The price ranges reflect *retail prices* that one can expect to pay for similar pieces in antiques shops across the country.

We have had a wonderful time creating this book. Almost every aspect of the Victorian era is fascinating, especially the decorative arts. Social customs, expanding technologies, the story of 19th-century immigrants—all shaped the evolution of furniture in Victorian America in interesting ways. We hope our book adds to your understanding and appreciation of this fascinating period of American furniture, and we hope it adds to your confidence in collecting Victorian furniture.

1

Gothic Revival

1830–1850

The Gothic Revival had its roots in 18th-century English Romanticism, with its love of the picturesque and the unusual. English designers of this persuasion felt that houses should be designed in harmony with their natural surroundings, and the results would be more picturesque if those surroundings were wild and scenic. Houses, like the landscape, should exhibit plenty of variety, contrast, a sense of movement, and even surprise. It was felt that Gothic architecture, one of the glories of England's past, best captured the picturesque aesthetic. Probably the best-known example of Gothic Revival architecture from the mid-18th century was Horace Walpole's Strawberry Hill, while in furniture, the designs of Thomas Chippendale featured many Gothic motifs. But aside from a few motifs in American Chippendale furniture, the Gothic Revival did not come to America until the 1820s and '30s, where it was first seen in church architecture. By the 1830s it was more widespread as an architectural style, with furniture also designed to complement it.

Architectural Antecedents and Furniture Makers

How were Gothic designs transmitted from England to America? The Englishman Robert Smith published *The Cabinet Maker and Upholsterer's Guide* in 1826 and it was filled with designs that could be produced for the middle class. The furniture included Gothic motifs such as arches, clustered columns, trefoils and quatrefoils, crockets and finials. Robert Conner, also English, borrowed from some of these designs, and published them in New York in 1842 in his book *The Cabinet Maker's Assistant.*[1]

Alexander Jackson Davis is probably the best-known American architect who designed Gothic Revival houses, the most famous being Glen Ellen in Baltimore (built in 1832) and Lyndhurst in Tarrytown, New York (built for New York mayor William Paulding in 1838). Davis's 1838 publication, *Rural Residences,* encouraged rural Gothic architecture—

---

1. Robert C. Smith, "Gothic and Elizabethan Revival Furniture, 1800–1850," *The Magazine Antiques* 75 (March 1959): 275.

houses that were meant to fit into the landscape and echo its picturesque qualities. These houses included features like gables, carved vergeboards, turrets, pinnacles, battlements, and tinted windows.[2] Bringing all these features together resulted in a varied outline—an interesting silhouette that was indeed unpredictable. The Hudson River Valley probably had the densest population of Gothic Revival homes. During the 1830s the American authors James Fenimore Cooper and Washington Irving built and added Gothic touches to their homes in New York State. Cooper turned his Otsego Hall into a Gothic mansion, and Irving created his Sunnyside on the Hudson River.

Davis designed furniture to go with his Gothic Revival houses, and the furniture was executed by New York cabinetmakers, such as Alexander Roux and the firm of Burns & Trainque. The best Gothic Revival furniture was often designed by architects, and much of this furniture is now in museums, or if not, is eagerly sought by specialized collectors. The motifs used on furniture were somewhat different from those found on architecture, although the furniture—like the architecture—is distinguished by the use of arches, clustered columns, trefoils and quatrefoils, crockets and finials.

Andrew Jackson Downing, a landscape gardener who worked with Davis and who helped popularize the movement, noted the furniture style in his 1850 publication *The Architecture of Country Houses,* which included designs for elaborate Gothic villas and modest cottages. Downing praised the work of Burns & Trainque and the firm of Alexander Roux, saying "The most correct Gothic furniture

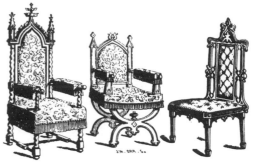

Fig. 1-1 Gothic Revival chairs, c. 1850, from A. J. Downing's *The Architecture of Country Houses* (1850). Downing writes, "Drawing-room and library chairs in the Gothic style are generally expensive and elaborate, being covered with rich stuffs, and highly carved." He also hints at a weakness of the style. The chair on the left, he says, "is too elaborate and ecclesiastical in character for most private houses. . . . We much prefer, when richness is requisite, to get it, in Gothic furniture, by covering rather plain and simple designs with rich stuffs rather than by the exhibition of elaborate Gothic carving, the effect of which is usually rather severe and angular, when applied to furniture."

that we have seen in this county is by Burns and Tranque [sic], Broadway, New York. Some excellent specimens may also be seen at Roux."[3]

The firm of J. and J. W. Meeks of New York City produced much fine Gothic furniture in the 1830s and '40s. The Meeks firm took a different approach to the Gothic Revival than architect-designers did. Meek's furniture was generally based on late Empire forms which showed off richly figured veneers and was highlighted by Gothic accents. This combination was especially successful on large case pieces such as secretary/bookcases. An indication of the company's prestige

2. Katherine S. Howe and David B. Warren, *The Gothic Revival Style in America, 1830–1870* (Houston: Museum of Fine Arts, 1976), 1.

3. Andrew Jackson Downing, *The Architecture of Country Houses* (New York: D. Appleton, 1850; reprint, New York: Dover Publications, 1969), 440.

is the fact that the White House ordered Gothic chairs from them between 1845 and 1849. These chairs, which were of simple design with four Gothic arches and three trefoils incorporated into the backs, were later used during Lincoln's administration in the Cabinet Room.[4] Meeks's furniture was very well made and still finds a good market today.

John Jelliff of Newark, New Jersey, was best known for his Renaissance Revival furniture, but he did make Gothic Revival furniture as well, mainly in rosewood and walnut.

Form and Function

Gothic Revival pieces from the first half of the 19th century did not revive Gothic furniture forms but simply displayed Gothic motifs—crockets and finials, arches, tracery, trefoils and quatrefoils, and rose windows—on contemporary furniture forms. Aside from pieces designed by architects like Davis, cabinetmakers like the Meeks firm added Gothic details to late Empire designs, creating pieces that were subtly Gothic. This is the kind of furniture we are likely to find outside of museums.

In general, during this period, Gothic Revival furniture was considered most suitable for the library, halls, and sometimes for the dining room. Gothic furniture for halls included hall chairs with hinged seats, the lids lifting up for storage of small items like gloves. Hall chairs often with unupholstered wooden seats, were primarily ceremonial and decorative and not intended for lengthy sitting.

As interesting as this furniture is, even writers from the period felt that heavily Gothicized furniture was really not suited for most homes. A. J. Downing, for instance, found it too angular and not domestic in feeling. He wrote, "We much prefer, when richness is requisite, to get it, in Gothic furniture, by covering rather plain and simple designs with rich stuffs, rather than by the exhibition of elaborate Gothic carving, the effect of which is usually rather severe and angular, when applied to furniture."[5] Downing much pre-

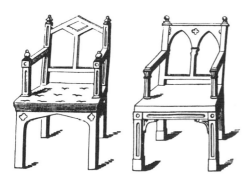

Fig. 1-2 Two Gothic Revival chairs, c. 1850, from Downing's *The Architecture of Country Houses* (1850). He promotes these because they are relatively simple and can be made fairly easily. He recommends them for the hall or living room.

Fig. 1-3 Gothic Revival bed, c. 1850, from Downing's book. Very popular with certain collectors today, this "sanctified" bed was a rarity even in the period.

---

4. John N. Pearce and Lorraine W. Pearce, "More on the Meeks Cabinetmakers," *The Magazine Antiques* 90 (July 1966): 70–73.

[5]Downing, 447–48.

ferred plainer Gothic furniture that could be made by local carpenters or cabinet-makers. Simply by adding a few Gothic details to sturdy rectilinear forms, one could make furniture that was functional and stylish—and not the special preserve of the wealthy.

Gothic Revival furniture was found not only in homes but also in many of the Gothic Revival churches that proliferated in 19th-century America. In fact, churches have continued to demand it throughout the 20th century. Apart from choir stalls, altars, and church pews, one often finds on the market today Gothic thrones or bishops' chairs, which originally would have been in a church.

One final note about Gothic Revival furniture from the 1830s and '40s: it is not to be confused with "Modern Gothic" furniture of the 1870s and '80s. The later Modern Gothic can be distinguished by the inclusion of shallow, incised carving of geometric forms and stylized floral designs, along with Gothic motifs. It is related to the designs of Charles Eastlake and Bruce Talbert, but more on that in Chapter 6.

Gothic Revival oak hall chair, c. 1850, not designed for comfort but for ornament. Wooden seat lifts for storage of small items like gloves. Gothic pierced back. Spool-turned legs. 18″ wide × 17½″ deep × 43½″ high. *Private collection.* **$350–450**.

Gothic hybrid carved walnut armchair, c. 1860, with spired crest surmounted with finials and pierced with quatrefoil above upholstered oval back, joined with open armrest continuing to a shaped seat frame raised on ring-turned legs. The spool turnings are typical of a midcentury look. This may have been made for a church. *Courtesy Neal Auction Company, New Orleans, Nicholay & Morgan photographers.* **$1,000–1,500**.

Pair of walnut Gothic Revival side chairs, c. 1850, each back rising to a pointed arch enclosing Gothic tracery. With turned stiles and legs. *Courtesy Neal Auction Company, New Orleans, Nicholay & Morgan photographers.* **$650–950** the pair.

Good Gothic Revival oak armchair, c. 1850, probably made in New York. With well-turned double-spiral legs and stiles. Back with "rose window," Gothic arches, quatrefoil, crest with crockets and fleur-de-lys finial. On rollers. Tufted seat. Original condition, old finish. *Courtesy Neal Auction Company, New Orleans, Nicholay & Morgan photographers.* **$1,800–3,000**.

Pair of rosewood Gothic Revival side chairs, c. 1855, attributed to Thomas Brooks, Brooklyn, N.Y. Relatively simple design with cutout quatrefoils and trefoils, fleur-de-lys finials. On rollers. 46¼″ high × 19″ wide × 18″ deep. *Courtesy Neal Auction Company, New Orleans, Nicholay & Morgan photographers.* **$750–1,250** the pair.

Gothic Revival dresser, c. 1840, based on a late Empire/Restauration design featuring flame mahogany veneers, with a few Gothic touches. Two over three drawers. Two glove boxes with cabinets above with glazed, pointed-arch doors and fleur-de-lys finials. Mirror also with fleur-de-lys finial. *Courtesy Flomaton Antique Auction, Flomaton, Ala.* **$1,800–2,400**.

Gothic-Empire mahogany cabinet, c. 1840. Molded frieze over one cupboard door, flanked by curved sides and scrolling stiles. Scroll feet. Typically extravagant use of flame mahogany in this Restauration-Gothic hybrid. 30½″ wide × 17¾″ deep × 39″ high. *Courtesy Frank H. Boos Auction Gallery, Bloomfield Hills, Mich.* **$1,000–1,500**.

Gothic Revival wardrobe, c. 1850, featured in Downing's book. He believed this type of simple but attractive furniture could be available to the general public, and he championed many of these straightforward designs.

Gothic Revival rosewood library table, c. 1840–50. Inset marble top above a shaped apron with reticulated border, resting on bracketed cusp-carved supports containing pierced Gothic panels, joined with an arched stretcher. 29½″ high × 49″ wide × 25″ deep. *Courtesy Neal Auction Company, New Orleans, Nicholay & Morgan photographers.* **$4,000–6,000**.

Gothic Revival carved oak library table, c. 1850, with variegated inset marble top with outset corners. Conforming apron decorated with quatrefoils and foliated medallions. Raised on an arched trestle-form base, architecturally buttressed by a span of Romanesque arches. 34¾″ high × 83″ wide × 35″ deep. *Courtesy Neal Auction Company, New Orleans, Nicholay & Morgan photographers.* **$7,000–10,000**.

Gothic Revival carved rosewood library table, c. 1845, by J. and J. W. Meeks (labeled). Marble top with rounded corners and molded edge above pierce-carved quatrefoil frieze, raised on scrolled legs joined by a scrolled stretcher, mounted at the intersections with turned finials, ending in scrolled feet on rectangular pads, casters. 41″ long × 30¼″ high. *Courtesy Butterfield & Butterfield, Los Angeles.* **$8,000–12,000.**

A highly important rosewood Gothic Revival center table attributed to A. J. Davis, c. 1840. Pie-veneered top, frieze with wave molding, beading, and Gothic arches alternating with drop finials. Very distinctive base with six columns joined by Gothic arches and trefoils, resting on pie-veneered base with three feet terminating in Gothic trefoils. This piece has it all—excellent provenance, association with the founder of the Gothic Revival movement in America, very good condition—all the drop finials (acorns) are original (this may sound insignificant, but it is crucial to the integrity of a fine piece). These factors have a strong impact on value. *Courtesy Joan Bogart, Rockville Centre, N.Y.* Dealer estimate: **$30,000–50,000** plus (depending on condition).

Gothic Revival mahogany double-door armoire, c. 1840. Projecting molded cornice with rounded corners, above a pair of generously proportioned doors displaying inset Gothic-arch panels, opening to a well-fitted interior with graduated drawers and pull-out slides. On conforming base with short vasiform-turned feet. Original untouched finish, as found. *Courtesy Neal Auction Company, New Orleans, Nicholay & Morgan photographers.* **$2,000–3,000.**

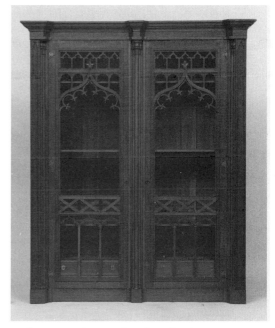

Walnut Gothic Revival double-door bookcase, c. 1860. Cornice with chamfered crenelated blocks above an applied Gothic fretwork frieze. Glazed doors with Gothic tracery carving and the sides with applied fretwork. Plinth base. 71″ high × 52″ wide × 12″ deep. *Courtesy Neal Auction Company, New Orleans, Nicholay & Morgan photographers.* **$1,500–2,400.**

Gothic Revival carved walnut bookcase, c. 1840, with molded, projecting cornice above cluster columns. Two doors with Gothic tracery. Inside are shelves and a pair of drawers below. Plinth base. 95″ high × 72″ wide × 21″ deep. *Courtesy Neal Auction Company, New Orleans, Nicholay & Morgan photographers.* **$3,500–5,500.**

A magnificent Gothic Revival bookcase, c. 1840, of mahogany and mahogany veneers. Breakfront form, with four drawers in base. Doors with Gothic arches and quatrefoil mullions. Pediment with band of acorn and leaf carving. Made by Richard Byrne of White Plains, New York, who is known to have executed designs by A. J. Davis for the Gothic mansion *Lyndhurst*. This piece has been in the *Lyndhurst* area since it was made and has a closely documented provenance, including families of note and even the name of the railroad station where the piece was originally delivered. The documented maker, wonderful form and excellent provenance enrich the value of the piece. *Courtesy of Joan Bogart, Rockville Centre, N.Y.* Dealer estimate: **$40,000–50,000**.

Gothic Revival carved mahogany bedstead, c. 1840. Flamboyant headboard in a highly stylized Gothic manner, yet held within a traditional set of columns and connecting boards such as were used from 1825–1865. *Courtesy New Orleans Auction Gallery, New Orleans.* **$3,500–5,000.**

Empire secretary with Gothic Revival touches by the Meeks firm, c. 1845. Typical of Empire furniture is the flame mahogany veneer and ogee cornice. The Gothic touches are seen in the arched mullions and arched interior door executed in crossbanding. *Courtesy Morton Goldberg Auction Galleries, New Orleans.* **$4,500–6,500.**

Imposing Gothic Revival carved mahogany full-tester bed, c. 1850. Deeply molded tester with applied cornice beading and richly carved acanthus leaves, with lacy arcaded gallery. Spiral-turned posts topped by carved capitals and resting on Gothicized blocks carved in full relief with figures in Renaissance dress holding symbolic objects, each standing within a Gothic arch on plinth base. Pierce-carved crested headboard panelled with blind fretwork and extensive Gothic tracery, which is also found on the rails and footboard. A commissioned tour de force by a master cabinetmaker. From a Gothic mansion in New Orleans. *Courtesy Neal Auction Gallery, New Orleans, Nicholay & Morgan photographers.* **$25,000–35,000.**

Gothic Revival mahogany hall tree, c. 1845–60, with mirror, knobs for hats/coats/umbrellas, cast iron drip pan with shell motif, pierce-carved back featuring fleur-de-lys-type shapes. 7' high. *Private collection.* **$1,200–1,500**.

Gothic Revival cast iron umbrella stand and rack, c. 1850, with repeated Gothic arches and cluster columns, quatrefoils, and fleur-de-lys finials. The Gothic Revival style was very popular with the cast iron manufacturers. 30" wide × 12" × 70½" high. *Courtesy New Orleans Auction Gallery, New Orleans.* **$1,500–2,500**.

2

Cottage Furniture
1840–1890

It might be said that cottage furniture was the poor man's answer to Gothic furniture. Coming on the heels of the Gothic Revival period, cottage furniture also was rooted in a past style, being an economical interpretation of Elizabethan designs. It was inexpensive furniture, but it also could be quite charming. It was meant for simple cottages, bedrooms or other private areas of the house, or servants' quarters.

A. J. Downing reserved special praise for cottage furniture in his 1850 book *The Architecture of Country Houses.* A champion of unpretentious furniture and an influential taste maker, he even made several suggestions for creating one's own pretty furniture out of barrels, whose curves could be made into chair backs or settee backs, with ruffled skirts added to make a charming chair. Downing's suggestions remind us of the state of the furniture trade in America at midcentury. Not everyone had access to "store-bought" furniture. In rural areas or newly settled areas, or for frugality, many still depended on the skills of a family member for at least some of their furniture. If a family had only a few dollars to spend, "store bought" cottage furniture was the least expensive around.

Design Elements

Downing mentioned Edward Hennessey of Boston as being one of the best makers of cottage furniture: "This furniture is remarkable for its combination of lightness and strength, and its essentially cottage-like character. It is very highly finished, and is usually painted drab, white, grey, a delicate lilac, or a fine blue—the surface polished and hard, like enamel."[1]

Less-expensive suites were made of pine or some other soft wood and were painted as Downing described. Especially early in the period, more expensive pieces were made of mahogany or other hardwoods. These might be more elaborately decorated and have marble surfaces.

As can be seen from the Hennessey suite in Fig. 2-1, one of the chief characteristics of cottage furniture is spool or bobbin turning. This kind of decoration,

---

1. Andrew Jackson Downing, *The Architecture of Country Houses* (New York: D. Appleton, 1850; reprint New York: Dover Publications, 1969), 415.

Fig. 2-1 Cottage bedroom suite in an Elizabethan style, c. 1850, from A. J. Downing's *The Architecture of Country Houses*. This set, made by the Hennessey firm of Boston, was available "in dark wood, or tastefully painted, the ground of drab, enriched with well-executed vignettes in the panels, and marble tops to the principle articles, at from $70 to $100 the set, including 4 chairs." Today, a full set: **$1,800–2,400**. Chest: **$450–650**. Washstand: **$350–475**. Bed: **$275–475**. Bedside cabinet: **$400–600**. Chair: **$125–225**.

which could be inexpensively produced with the multiple-bladed lathe, had associations with the past and was seen as a variation of the barley-twist or spiral turnings on Elizabethan furniture. Elizabethan

furniture, Downing felt, had a picturesque beauty, with its twisted legs, fringes, and quaint carving. As charming as Elizabethan furniture was, cottage furniture was even more so because it was available to everyone.

The picturesque charm of this kind of furniture being conceded, to what, then, is it owing? We think, to the domestic feeling which pervades it. . . . It has a homey strength and sober richness. . . . It is undeniable that, to the present age, the charm of this antique furniture is in its romance—in its long association with times, events, and names that have a historical interest, and that move our feelings deeply by means of such powerful associations. . . . It is so much richer and more domestic than strictly Gothic furniture, that it will always be preferred to the latter by most persons."[2]

Cottage furniture was especially popular for bedrooms, and the spool-turned bed got a boost from a brush with celebrity. The association with the beloved Swedish singer surely increased the popularity of the spool-turned "Jenny Lind" bed during the second half of the 19th century.

Factory Production

Cottage furniture in the spool or Elizabethan style was a snap to manufacture using the earliest steam-driven machines. Circular saws and lathes were among the first woodworking tools to be harnessed to steam power. The steam-driven lathe could make the spool or bobbin turnings with ease, and the circular saw greatly sped up the cutting of boards. These two processes were about all that was needed to make a Jenny Lind–type bed.

There were many large factories in Chicago, Baltimore, Grand Rapids and other cities that made cottage furniture

and shipped it all over the country by boat and railroad.

Cottage furniture was the least-expensive mass-produced furniture available until the golden oak period, when the mail-order giants made affordable, sturdy, oak pieces in fanciful styles to the delight of households throughout America. Until then, cottage furniture was a given, maintaining its overall simplicity and affordability, while subtly adapting a silhouette and painting style to reflect the latest fashion.

2. Ibid, 451 (italics his).

Cottage bedroom suite, c. 1850, featured in A. J. Downing's *The Architecture of Country Houses*. He gives the original price for this set, which was made by Edward Hennessey, as $36—one of his least-expensive sets! Today, a full set: **$1,000–1,500**. Washstand: **$275–475**. Chair: **$100–150**. Bed: **$300–475**. Dressing table: **$300–475**.

Seven-piece New England painted cottage bedroom set in the Eastlake style, c. 1870. With floral and bird designs centering landscapes accented by pinstripes on light gray-green background. *Courtesy Skinner, Inc., Boston, Mass.* Bed: **$450–600**. Dresser: **$500–750**. Washstand: **$350–450**. Table: **$150–225**. Chair: **$75–125**. As a set: **$2,500–3,500**.

Child's chair, c. 1860, with spool-turned legs, stiles and spindles. Crest rail and base of back with faint remains of stencilled decoration. Caned seat. Very similar in style to the Hennessey sets—typical, charming cottage furniture. *Private collection.* **$75–125**.

Cottage bedroom suite, c. 1850, from A. J. Downing's book *The Architecture of Country Houses*. This set (with four chairs) "without marble tops, but highly finished 'china white, peach blossom, or blue ground, single gilt lines, ornamented,' is $68. The same, with marble top to several of the articles, $80. The wardrobe shown is $18 more." Today, a full set: **$5,000–6,000**. Washstand: **$600–900**. Dresser: **$1,000–1,500**. Bedside cabinet: **$500–750**. Sleigh bed: **$1,000–1,500**. Towel rack: **$100–150**. Chair: **$175–275**. Table: **$175–350**. Wardrobe: **$1,800–2,500**.

Faux rosewood (maple) "Grecian" rocker, c. 1860. A caned rocker like this most likely would have been kept in the bedroom. 41″ high. *Private collection.* **$275–375**.

Child's caned "Grecian" rocker, c. 1860, rocker with scrolling arms, shaped seat and crest rail. *Private collection.* **$125–175.**

Boston rocker, c. 1830–60. Crest rail with stencilled landscape. The Boston rocker, probably the earliest rocking chair form—dating from around 1825—was popular throughout the century. The rocking chair originated in America, unlike many of the other popular Victorian furniture forms. 40" high. *Courtesy Butte's Antiques, Oxford, N.C.* **$250–450.**

Walnut table, c. 1860, with shaped molded top with drop finials, turned legs, trestle base with shaped shelf stretcher. 33" long × 18½" wide × 29½" high. *Private collection.* **$175–275.**

Table, c. 1860, with shaped top, drop finials, turned legs, trestle base, shelf stretcher. Soft wood with ebonized finish. 15" wide x 26" long x 28½" high. Private collection **$125–175.**

Walnut Elizabethan Revival cottage table, c. 1860, with spool-turned legs on trestle base. 19″ long × 15″ wide × 26″ high. *Private collection.* **$75–125**.

Elizabethan Revival parlor table, c. 1860, with marble turtle-shaped top. Apron with flame mahogany veneer, beading and drop finials. Shelf also accented with beading. Legs and stretchers spool turned. Sides with fret-carved scrolling decoration. Fancy cottage furniture. 29½″ long × 17½″ deep × 29″ high. *Private collection.* **$450–650**.

Cottage pine chest, c. 1860, with original painted and gilt stencilled decoration. Original white marble top of bowed form with conforming top drawer over three drawers. Restoration overtones in the feet and decoration. Original wood pulls. *Private collection.* **$900–1,200**.

Black-painted pine cottage washstand, c. 1870, with stencilled decoration of graceful swirls and fruit. Scalloped, molded backsplash, molded top. One drawer over cabinet. Scalloped apron. Drawer with "button and scallop" dovetails (produced by the Knapp dovetailing machine, invented 1868). 24″ high. *Courtesy The Antique Mall, Hillsborough, N.C.* **$300–475**.

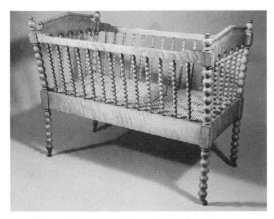

Spool-turned tiger maple and maple crib, c. 1870, with turned spindles and legs, casters, 42¼″ long × 24″ wide × 34″ high. *Courtesy Frank H. Boos Auction Gallery, Bloomfield Hills, Mich.* **$800–1,200.**

Cottage bedroom suite in the Renaissance Revival style, c. 1865. Bed with panelled headboard, finials, Renaissance-type cartouche, painted outlines and painted floral decorations. Matching dresser with candle stands, marble surfaces, original drop pulls on lower drawers. Matching washstand with marble backsplash, brackets and top, with one drawer over cabinets. With original drop pulls. *Private collection.* The set, **$3,500–4,500.**

3

Rococo Revival
1840–1865

If cottage furniture was homey and domestic, rococo furniture met another need: it was elegant and feminine and had the status associated with all things French. If cottage furniture was for the private parts of the house, rococo was for the most public parts. In 1850 a parlor furnished with Rococo Revival furniture told visitors that the homeowners were "au courant" with the latest fashions. The Rococo Revival reached its peak of popularity in the years immediately preceding the Civil War. Inspired by 18th-century French designs, the Rococo Revival was marked by curving forms—including C-scrolls, S-scrolls, and cabriole legs—and high-relief sculptural carving of fruit, vegetables and flowers. The curving forms could be as simple as the ubiquitous balloon-back lady's chair or as complex as the parlor sofa with triple-arching back or the S-shaped *têtc-à-tête*. Serpentine drawer fronts and sofa seat rails completed the theme. The best pieces used rosewood, though mahogany was also used, especially on earlier pieces, and walnut was widely used on less-expensive furniture. The better pieces had truly remarkable masses of carving, extravagant curves and rich upholstery.

With obvious design links to 18th-century French furniture, the style was called by an array of names in America—Antique French, Modern French, Louis XV and Louis XIV. None of these names is precisely accurate, but certainly the style does recall the sensuous curves of Louis XV Rococo furniture, a testament to the fact that at midcentury, France still dominated the decorative arts and had a rich cultural heritage that was envied by the young American nation. Even in America, French designers provided many of the best designs. In the aftermath of the revolutions of 1848, cabinetmakers and woodworkers emigrated in great numbers from France and Germany to the United States. Their presence contributed significantly to the character of American Victorian furniture.

Design Elements

Elegant rococo furniture suited the Victorian mindset in several ways. Just as 18th-century France had developed a number of new furniture forms—each with a specialized use—Rococo Revival furniture also presented several new forms, commonly given French names in deference to their heritage. The *tête-à-tête*, the *chaise légère* (reception chair), the gentleman's and lady's chairs (or *fauteuils*) from the standard parlor suite—each had a specific purpose and fit the Victorian need for hierarchy and order. One piece was for intimate conversation, one a formal piece for the hall, one for the man of the house, and one—smaller and more delicate—for the lady. Refinement, proof of man's progress, was expressed in terms of particular pieces of furniture for particular uses. It was also expressed in self control (mastery over complicated social rituals), control over natural resources and mastery over machines. There was attention to detail, from how one conducted oneself in social situations to how furniture was made. In furniture, refinement meant highly finished and polished surfaces, rich fabrics used in tufted upholstery, high-relief carving with realistic portrayals of the natural world and bountiful decoration. The French background of the Rococo Revival style greatly enhanced this sense of civilized refinement.[1]

Even though the curving lines owe an obvious debt to 18th-century French furniture, there are important differences. Eighteenth-century French furniture was lighter in weight and color, with chairs often painted in pastel colors. It had a delicate feeling, which was well suited to leisured court society. Flowers and foliage were used as decorative touches, but the effect was stylized and suggestive rather than strictly literal. In the 18th century, a simple flower or bit of foliage would suffice. The sensibility of 19th-century Rococo Revival pieces placed a premium on very realistic and detailed high-relief naturalistic carving. Nature was reproduced abundantly in great heavy masses of carving, including fruit, grapes and vines, foliage and even animals (see in particular the work of Belter, and some of the re-

markable sideboards illustrated in this chapter). Also, the Rococo style used *asymmetry* to create a whimsy, a constant visual delight and a lightness which is deeply contrasted with the balance and symmetry so important to the Victorian mind as it reinterpreted the 18th century into a modern sensibility. Symmetry speaks of control, perfection, strength—the dominant social goals of the 19th century.[2] Nineteenth-century Victorian furniture featured dark wood, such as walnut, mahogany or rosewood, with white marble for flat surfaces, expressing the Victorian love of contrast. This furniture obviously has a heavier, truly massive feeling. It is aggressive and ostentatious in its display of American wealth and bounty. It is vigorous and exuberant, whereas the French 18th-century Rococo is more delicate and graceful. So the Rococo Revival movement was much more than a backward-looking revival; it had a vitality and energy of its own that expressed the confidence of America at midcentury.

Although the Rococo Revival style had its finest flowering in America, this revival began in Europe and then made its way to America through immigrant cabinetmakers, style books and other means. Rococo Revival styles were popular in England and France by the 1820s, perhaps in reaction to the rather severe Empire style. On the Continent, the beginning of the reign of Charles X (1824) marks the beginning of the style. It also caught on in Germany, where the young John Henry Belter would have been exposed to it before he emigrated to America.

American cabinetmakers sold several types of Rococo Revival furniture. Some they imported from France, others they copied from the imports or based on French style books. We know something about the experience of one prominent

---

1. Katherine Grier, *Culture and Comfort: A Social History of Design from 1830–1900.* (Amherst: University of Massachusetts Press, 1988), 140–141.

2. For further discussion of 18th-century rococo, see Lindquist and Warren, *English and Continental Furniture with Prices* (Radnor, Pa.: Wallace-Homestead, 1994), 30–31.

cabinetmaking firm in Philadelphia, George Henkels, who advertised almost exact copies of furniture also found in the leading French furniture publications. It is quite possible that other cabinetmakers also produced copies of designs published in France. Sources of design included imported French furniture and French periodicals focusing on furnishings. Henkels lifted Rococo Revival designs straight out of French furniture publications from the 1840s and '50s. Apparently, Henkels also imported the latest French furniture for sale in his showrooms. In fact, it is difficult to know which of Henkels's pieces he produced himself and which were imported from France.[3]

Another means of spreading the popularity of Rococo Revival designs to the general public was the popular women's magazine *Godey's Magazine and Lady's Book*, published in Philadelphia. During the 1850s new French furniture forms and the rococo style in general were frequently discussed and clearly viewed as a desirable, stylish look.

The international exhibitions beginning in 1851 were another important way to transmit design ideas from Europe to America. They also served as an important venue for various countries to compete with each other—national rivalries ran high, fueled by a resentment against the long-standing dominance of French design. The London Crystal Palace Exhibition of 1851 and the Crystal Palace Exhibition in 1853 and 1854 in New York City displayed the latest in technology and design innovation for all the world to see. Rococo Revival was one of the major styles on display. Among the American firms documented as showing Rococo Revival pieces at the New York exhibition were Alexander Roux, A. Eliaers of Boston, Jules Dessoir, and John Henry Belter.

The popularity of the style was no doubt increased by its inclusion in the 1850 book *The Architecture of Country Houses* by influential tastemaker Andrew Jackson Downing. Downing had this recommendation for Rococo furniture:

Modern French furniture, and especially that in the style of Louis Quatorze, stands much higher in general estimation in this country than any other. Its union of lightness, elegance, and grace renders it especially the favorite of the ladies. . . . The style of Louis XIV is characterized by greater delicacy of foliage ornamentation and greater intricacy of detail. We may add to this, that besides elegance of most French drawing-room furniture, its superior workmanship, and the luxurious ease of its admirably constructed seats, strongly commend it to popular favor.[4]

Parlor Furniture

Destined to grace the parlor, rococo furniture was often produced in parlor suites that fit a standard formula: sofa, gentleman's chair, smaller lady's chair and four side chairs, which were arranged in an ordered, symmetrical manner (Figs. 3-1 to 3-3). These suites usually matched exactly, or if not, were closely related in decorative motifs and certainly all upholstered with the same fabric. At midcentury, elegance and formality were expressed not only in voluptuous carving and curves, but also in a sense of order expressed in the matching suite—a notion that became somewhat hackneyed by the end of the century. These suites were grouped around the ubiquitous center table, which generally did not match the seating furniture but

---

3. Kenneth L. Ames, "Designed in France: Notes on the Transmission of French Styles to America," *Winterthur Portfolio* 12 (1977): 104–110.

4. Andrew Jackson Downing, *The Architecture of Country Houses* (New York: D. Appleton, 1850; reprint, New York: Dover Publications, 1969), 432.

Fig. 3-1 Rosewood Rococo Revival seven-piece parlor suite, c. 1850–60, consisting of triple-back settee, two armchairs and four side chairs, each medallion back with fruit and nut rocaille crest carved in full relief, having out-carved arms and serpentine skirts. On cabriole legs. Settee is 41″ high × 63½″ long × 24″ deep. *Courtesy Neal Auction Company, New Orleans, Nicholay & Morgan photographers.* **$6,500–9,500** the set.

Fig. 3-3 Lady's and gentleman's chairs from the set.

Fig. 3-2 Four side chairs from the set.

was suited in character. One reason for the prominence of the center table was that before the days of electricity the family would gather together after dark around the lamp on the center table—the main source of light by which to read or sew. Perhaps this was another way of maintaining family bonds that were so important in Victorian society.

Victorians considered the parlor part of the woman's domain, best furnished with feminine furniture; Rococo Revival was perfect. High-backed chairs made by Belter and others were stylish. The Victorians loved the dramatic form, even though it weakened the structure. In fact, this might be taken as a general rule for Victorian furniture: visual qualities took precedence over solid construction. Since formality was a prime consideration for parlor suites, most did not include rockers since they were usually considered too informal. A Victorian writer cautioned against their use in 1840: "Swaying backwards and forwards in a parlour rocking chair is a most ungraceful recreation, particularly for a lady . . . and very annoying to spectators, who may happen to be a little nervous."[5]

Upholstery was naturally an important part of the parlor suite, being a means to make all the pieces match as well as a way to make a suite more lavish and expensive. The complex curving forms of rococo furniture seemed to demand rich upholstery. The best Rococo Revival parlor suites had elaborate tufted upholstery, which required a great deal of hand work. The fine fabric and the amount of workmanship added to the final cost of the furniture. As the 19th century progressed, machines were saving more and more money on furniture production, but the money saved could easily be spent on lavish upholstery. So in many cases, although machines took over the carving and joining of the furniture, almost as much total handwork went into a piece in the form of upholstery—an area where it was easy to indulge in "conspicuous consumption." The choice of upholstery could make a statement about the cost of the piece as well as the taste and economic status of its owner.

By this time, coil spring upholstery was no longer thought of as an aid for the infirm or aged, as it had first been conceived. The level of comfort created by coil springs was now felt to be fitting for the parlor. Even though these pieces do not approach the comfort of 20th-century overstuffed furniture, they were a real improvement over stuffed seats supported by webbing alone.

When we think about this formal and decorative furniture, it is helpful to consider the customs of the people using it. Women at this time suffered the constraints of corsets to shape their figures and voluminous skirts under which were worn stiff "cages" or hoops. Chairs for ladies were specifically designed with no arms or with modified arms to allow room for these full skirts. Depending on the type of corset worn, women could only perch on chairs; true relaxation was not an option in the formal parlor setting.

Men fared better; uncorsetted, they could at least lean back comfortably. The gentlemen's chairs also had arms and larger proportions. So if you entered a Victorian parlor furnished with a suite, you would know exactly where to sit based on your gender.

Cabinetmaking Firms

Since parlor life in Victorian America was so indebted to French culture, it is not surprising to learn that many of the leading designers of the most fashionable style were recent French immigrants. Most of the cabinetmakers from this era were French or German immigrants as well, who brought with them fine cabinetmaking skills and a familiarity with the latest European fashions. Much of the Rococo Revival furniture that can be attributed to a particular maker was produced by one of a number of firms that were based in New York City and had shops along a fashionable stretch of Broadway during the 1850s and '60s. Charles Bauduoine, John Henry Belter, Burns & Trainque, Alexander Roux, Julius Dessoir, Rochefort and Skarren, Pottier and Stymus, Ringuet Le Prince and Leon Marcotte

---

5. Eliza Leslie, *The Handbook: or a Manual of Domestic Economy* (Philadelphia: Carey and Hart, 1840), 198. Cited in Grier, *Culture and Comfort,* 109

were among this elite group. They employed highly skilled artisans—most of whom were recent immigrants—to do the crucial work by hand. This class of furniture was not mass-produced but made to order or made for limited stock. It is important to remember that even in New York City in the 1850s and '60s, steam-powered woodworking machinery was far from common. This was still an era that depended on hand craftsmanship on the best quality furniture.[6]

Aside from the prestigious firms, there was also a lower level of furniture manufacturers who were involved in wholesale manufacturing. They made furniture, primarily in suites, to be sold to dealers. There were many of these firms in what was known as "Little Germany" in New York City.[7] In 1853, 85% of the furniture made in New York was shipped out to the West and South, especially to New Orleans.

Obviously, most of the furniture on the market today comes from these wholesale manufacturers. When compared to furniture made by the finer firms, we can see that wholesale furniture used less expensive woods, and its decoration was less developed or less finished. Fine carving, then and now, must be done by hand; this kind of expense could not be justified on wholesale furniture.

John Henry Belter

John Henry Belter was born in 1804 in Germany, came to the United States in 1840 and worked in New York City from 1844 to 1863. He was among the wave of European immigrants who helped shape the look of American Victorian Furniture, and his work represents the height of the Rococo Revival style in all its exuberance. Although the 19th century is often branded as a time when technology triumphed at the expense of design, Belter's furniture represents a happy marriage of the two. His techniques for using laminated wood were perfect for the extravagantly curving surfaces so characteristic of Rococo Revival furniture. Belter used the same principles involved in making plywood to create some of the most stunning furniture of the 19th century.

Laminated wood is made of very thin sheets of wood that are glued together, usually with the grain of the wood at right angles, thus increasing strength. Laminated wood is actually stronger than solid wood of the same thickness, and it can be steamed and bent more easily than solid wood—it has both strength and flexibility. In the case of rosewood, which has a beautiful grain but is quite brittle in solid form, using it in laminated form has definite advantages. Belter was able to use surprisingly thin pieces of laminated rosewood and not only curve them but also pierce them extensively with his patented saws.

Belter generally used rosewood for the outer layer of veneer—the part that would be seen. His famous laminated process resulted in a final product (Belter called it "pressed work furniture") that was actually stronger than if it had been created out of solid rosewood. Although rosewood is what we associate with Belter's most characteristic pieces, he also used mahogany and even oak as primary woods. The use of mahogany may indicate work of an earlier date (the 1840s), when mahogany was still widely used and before the Rococo Revival style had peaked. In his 1858 patent he explained his use of veneers:

In short, the veneers . . . which, when the work is in place, are exhibited to the observer on the front side, and the veneers . . . which are shown

---

6. Katherine S. Howe et al. *Herter Brothers: Furniture and Interiors for a Gilded Age* (New York: Harry N. Abrams, 1994), 57–59.

7. Ibid., 60–61.

on the back side, should be rosewood, or the like highly-prized wood, while all the rest may be oak, hickory, black walnut, or other cheap wood.[8]

Belter used molds or cauls to shape the laminated wood as the glue dried, thus forming his famous sinuous shapes. Of course, he did not invent the process of laminating, nor of bending solid wood. He did, however, patent four devices and techniques that he used in conjunction with lamination to create his unique designs. The documentation for these patents has provided valuable information about Belter.

His first patent, in 1847, was for a special saw to pierce-carve chair backs. He titled it "Machinery for Sawing Arabesque Chairs." In 1856 he got another patent for his remarkable laminated bedstead, which could be constructed in two sections rather than the traditional four. A bedstead in two sections has a headboard that flows in one piece into side rails that extend one-half the normal length. The second piece consists of a footboard that also flows into its own partial side rails. The side rails are then joined together to form the bed (see color illustration).

In 1858 Belter received a patent for laminated chair backs made with cauls or molds. Chairs made by this process had backs that curved on two planes (cut not from a cylinder, but from a spherical mold). The efficiency of this operation was increased by the fact that Belter could cut eight chair backs out of one barrel-shaped mold.[9]

His final patent, granted in 1860, concerned the design of bureaus whose drawers were all cut from the same cylinder, thus assuring the absolute uniformity necessary for Belter's boldly curving surfaces. He also devised a system to lock all the drawers at one time.[10]

Collectors seek technical standards that will hold true for authenticating all Belter pieces. We have few of these rules, but furniture historians have been able to establish some facts about Belter's laminations. A high-power magnifier and very good ruler help to study his laminations which tended to be thinner and more numerous than his competitors'. In seating furniture, Belter's veneer varied from seven to nine layers, each with a thickness ranging between 0.05″ and 0.07″ (the average being 0.062″).[11] Laminations used to make tables were also about 0.06″, while those for beds were thicker, adding needed strength.[12]

Although we associate Belter's name with the lamination process, his output was not limited to this type of furniture. He is known to have made some pieces out of solid wood and also to have made others which combined laminated and solid wood. Some of his early chairs, for example, have applied solid crests which had been carved in high relief. On chairs, some side rails are solid and some veneer.[13]

It is sometimes said that one can identify a Belter chair because there will be no visible seam on the chair back. However, this is not necessarily true. If there is a visible seam, it will be vertical, and in some cases, veneers are lined up symmetrically along the seam to highlight strongly figured rosewood veneer.[14]

8. Marvin D. Schwarz et al, *The Furniture of John Henry Belter and the Rococo Revival* (New York: E. P. Dutton, 1981), 20.

9. Ibid., 28.

10. Ibid., 29.

11. Ibid., 16.

12. Ibid., 34.

13. Ibid., 15.

14. Ibid., 13.

Although some Belter seating furniture has plain, molded legs, most exhibit floral carving on the seat rail and legs, and as is generally true of Belter carving, it is more elaborate and realistic when compared to the stylized rendering of other makers. Rear legs generally had a noncircular (rectangularlike) cross section.[15]

Belter's tables were not made to match the chairs they accompanied. Generally, parlor furniture of this period included seating furniture and tables that were related but not strictly matched. Belter's parlor furniture generally had pierce-carved chairs that went with pierce-carved tables, and solid-carved tables that went with solid-carved chairs. As with other Belter pieces, there do not appear to be any simple, hard-and-fast rules that allow foolproof identification of his tables. Pierce-carved aprons were usually laminated, and solid wood was sometimes added on. He also made tables out of solid wood, laminated wood, or a combination of laminated and solid; in any case, his stretchers were *always* solid wood. Cauls were used to shape table aprons, just as they were used for chair backs.[16]

These general guidelines aside, recognizing Belter furniture is really a matter of being familiar with a large body of Rococo Revival furniture and then comparing known Belter examples. In most generic Rococo Revival furniture, C-scrolls and S-scrolls are prevalent and provide the framework for the other decorative motifs. Belter occasionally used such scrolls, but even more characteristic of his work, particularly in seating furniture, is the use of naturalistic motifs like branches or vines, either rendered realistically or in a more sinuous version (as in some of his slipper chairs). These naturalistic elements provide the framework for the rest of his carving, which includes acorns, grapes and other fruit. Stylistically, Belter's carving, with its striking sense of realism, stands out above the work of other shops. It is lifelike and not naive or stylized as in the case of lesser makers. Belter tables, like the chairs, do not incorporate as many C-scrolls and S-scrolls as are common with other makers of the period. Instead, the decoration is quite distinctive, with flowers, grape clusters, vines, leaves and branches that connect all of these elements.[17]

As with other 19th-century cabinetmakers, we are able to learn some details of his business life through city directories of the time. A telling detail in Belter's case is that his listing in New York directories changed around 1853, from the designation "cabinetmaker" to "manufacturer," indicating a shift in Belter's business from custom-made furniture to furniture produced on a larger scale and warehoused for future sale. His factory at 3rd Avenue and 76th Street opened in 1854.[18] Interestingly, although the scale of his business changed, he used many of the same patterns before and after he expanded his operations. The development of the various patterns remains something of a mystery. We do not know which came first, but once in use, they were made throughout his career and not set aside in favor of a new pattern.[19]

Naming Belter patterns is problematic since none of his actual pattern books or catalogs are available today. The only pattern for which a name was actually given by Belter comes from a bill of sale for a set of furniture with cornucopias and elaborate carving. In the 1855 bill made out to the Jordan family, the name "Arabasket" is used. Through common usage, names have become associated with several pat-

15. Ibid., 35–36, 10.
16. Ibid., 10, 20, 21.
17. Ibid., 10, 20.
18. Ibid., 28.
19. Ibid., 35 and 37.

terns of seating furniture. Tuthill King was named after a Chicago family. Rosalie—the most common Belter chair pattern—was named for a set bought for Rosalie Plantation in Natchez, Mississippi, around 1860. It is one of the simpler patterns, unpierced and with a crest of flowers and fruit, a molded frame and a filler of parallel lines with dots in between (see related pattern in Fig. 3-4). Henry Clay, named for a set at Ashland—Clay's home—is unpierced and has a solid, upholstered back framed by broad sweeping scrolls and surmounted by flowers.

Most of Belter's known work consists of parlor furniture. There are several possible reasons for this. By about 1850 the Renaissance Revival style was beginning to be popular in dining rooms; Belter may have used good business instincts and created a niche for his work in the parlors of America. In general, Rococo Revival furniture was considered best suited for the parlor, which was feminine territory in the Victorian home. Belter dining room furniture is rare indeed.[20]

Also rare, and truly remarkable, are the beds made by Belter. Because of the

Fig. 3-4 Rococo Revival rosewood side chair and armchair by John Henry Belter, New York City, c. 1845–65, in the pattern known as "Rosalie with Grapes"—one of Belter's most common patterns. Each with laminated back with large interconnected scrolling pieces topped by heavily carved crest with roses, grapes, foliage. Molded seat rails with scroll and rose carving. Cabriole legs, whorl feet with acanthus. On casters. *Private collection.* Side chair: **$1,200–1,800.** Armchair: **$4,000–6,000.**

20. Ibid., 35.

strength needed in a bed frame, Belter used 16 to 24 layers of veneer (more layers than he used for chairs and tables). The beds were supported on four or six feet, the two additional ones being in the center of each side rail. To a modern eye, the beds are perhaps his most appealing form because the decoration does not dominate, as is often the case with other Victorian furniture. Relying less on the elaborate pierced carving that characterizes his tables and seating furniture, the beds display gracefully curving expanses of figured veneer with a proportionally smaller amount of carving. The designs appear seamless and wonderfully organic. The curving form is clearly the most essential part of these remarkable designs which are not overburdened with carving. This said, collectors today tend to pay top dollar for beds with the most carving, particularly pierced carving. On the more spectacular forms, the beds are actually constructed in two connecting parts, rather than the usual arrangement of four separate parts—headboard, footboard and side rails. These two-part bedsteads are rarely found.

In recent years, Belter beds have made headlines in auction news. For example, a very fine Belter bed sold at Pettigrew Auction Company of Colorado Springs, Colorado, in July 1990 for $101,750. The market for Belter furniture peaked at exciting levels like these. The 1990s saw a decrease in prices—a Belter bed comparable to the one mentioned above sold in June 1993 at Pettigrew for a much lower $55,000.

In light of modern resale values, it is interesting to think about prices during Belter's time. Belter's work was expensive when it was made, just as it is today. Bills show that a Belter parlor suite was priced at $1,200, costly but comparable to prices for other top-quality New York City mak-

ers.[21] Before the war newly wealthy industrialists sought out Belter's luxurious furniture to enhance their status. Belter distributed his furniture to other retailers, and we know that there were buyers in Chicago, New York City, the Northeast, and some in the South.

Although we know that Belter furniture was used at the Rosalie Plantation, it is probably a mistake to think that the Deep South antebellum mansions were largely furnished with his pieces. This seems to be a widespread misconception, probably originating with the 1939 movies *Gone With The Wind, Jezebel* and *Song of the South,* whose sets were full of Belter-type furniture. In fact, the furniture for these movies was all brought in from other parts of the country (mainly the Northeast). Furthermore, the South was generally a little more conservative than other parts of the country, and Southerners might not have chosen something as flashy as Belter's furniture. If one wanted that kind of furniture, there were several excellent makers in nearby New Orleans. It is difficult to say which geographic areas originally favored Belter, but there is evidence that Southerners have been strong buyers of Belter only since the 1930s.[22]

Belter died in 1863 of tuberculosis, but his partners (the Springmeyer brothers—one of whom was his brother-in-law) carried on the business until 1867, when it finally failed. Many have speculated about the reasons for the failure: the business may have been doomed without Belter or perhaps his exuberant style was out of step with the nation's somber mood after the tragedy of the Civil War. Certainly, he was known exclusively for Rococo Revival furniture, and the style was on the wane after the war. In addition, the financial depression right after the war surely had adverse affects on the business.

---

21. Ibid., 2.
22. Ibid., 3.

J. and J. W. Meeks

There are a number of other well-known furniture makers from this period, many of whom were based in New York City. The work of J. and J. W. Meeks is often compared to Belter's because Meeks too used laminations and pierce-carving. The Meeks firm was active in New York City from 1797 to 1868; however, they did not limit sales to that city. They sold much of their furniture in showrooms around the country (particularly in New Orleans). During their existence, they made furniture in all the popular styles, including Rococo Revival. Some of their rococo furniture rivals that of John Henry Belter.

Perhaps their best-known pattern is "Hawkins," so named because of the set given by Meeks to his daughter on her marriage to a Mr. Hawkins in 1859 (See Figs. 3-5, 3-6 and 3-7). Chairs of this type exhibit a construction similar to Belter's, with molded, laminated rosewood used for the chair backs.[23]

Most of the Meeks furniture that is labeled is in the Empire style. Almost none of their Rococo Revival work is marked, but we presume it to be theirs because it is strongly attributed.[24] The rococo furni-

Fig. 3-5 Laminated rosewood sofa, c. 1850, attributed to J. & J. W. Meeks. "Hawkins" pattern, after the set made by the firm for a Meeks daughter's marriage to Dexter Hawkins. Pierce-carved back with scrolling grape vines framed by heavier molded scrolls. Central crest with floral carving. Shaped and molded apron with central carving. Molded cabriole legs on casters. 63″ long. *Courtesy Witherell Americana Auctions, Elk Grove, Calif.* Dealer estimate: **$6,000–9,000.**

---

23. John N. Pearce et al, "The Meeks Family of Cabinetmakers," *The Magazine Antiques* 85 (April 1964): 414–20.
24. Schwarz et al, 5.

Fig. 3-7 Laminated rosewood side chair, c. 1850, attributed to J. & J. W. Meeks in the "Hawkins" pattern. *Courtesy Witherell Americana Auctions, Elk Grove, Calif.* Dealer estimate: **$2,000–3,500**.

Fig. 3-6 Laminated rosewood armchair, c. 1850, attributed to J. & J. W. Meeks. This also in the "Hawkins" pattern. *Courtesy Witherell Americana Auctions, Elk Grove, Calif.* Dealer estimate: **$4,000–6,000**.

ture that is generally associated with them has thicker lamination than those used by Belter, although Meeks's Rococo Revival work was laminated and solid, just as Belter's was.

Alexander Roux

Alexander Roux worked in New York City from 1837 to 1881 and had a reputation as one of the finest cabinetmakers of the period (see Fig. 3-8). Roux apparently trained in Paris before coming to America, making the most of his French heritage at a time when it was highly valued. Like other cabinetmakers of French descent, he also imported French furniture.

He maintained close ties with his brother, a maker of fine furniture in Paris who sometimes sent pieces to America. Andrew Jackson Downing had high praise for Roux in his book *Architecture of Country Houses:*

In New York, the rarest and most elaborate designs, especially for drawing-room and library use, are to be found at the warehouse of Roux, in Broadway. . . . At the warehouse of Mr. A. Roux, Broadway, may be found a large collection of furniture for the drawing-room, library, etc.—the most tasteful designs of Louis Quatorze, Renaissance, Gothic, etc. to be found in the country. . . . The chairs and sofas are particularly elegant[25] (see Fig. 3-9).

---

25. Downing, 432.

Fig. 3-8 Rococo Revival étagère, c. 1850, of faux-bois rosewood, attributed to Alexander Roux. Topped off by a cartouche with carved maiden's head surmounted by scrolling foliage. Central mirror flanked by exuberantly scrolling mirrored panels (compare this treatment, which is Rococo in its graceful curves, to the less graceful cutouts of the Renaissance étagères). Resting on a serpentine molded marble base on conforming scrolling base. A handsome piece. *Courtesy New Orleans Auction Company, New Orleans.* **$5,000–7,500.**

was on the cutting edge of fashion, Roux apparently left laminated furniture to Belter and Meeks.

A Roux advertisement from 1859 suggests the scope of his thriving business:

We have now on hand a large and splendid assortment of Plain and Artistic Furniture, such as Rosewood, Buhl, Ebony, and Gilt, and Marqueterie of foreign and domestic woods, and are now prepared to execute all orders for the furnishing of Houses, such as Wood Mantel-Pieces, Wainscoating, Mirror-Frames, Cornices, and Cabinet-Work in general, in the best manner and at the lowest rates.[27]

By 1855 he employed 120 people. The business peaked in the 1870s and he retired in 1881, but a son carried on until 1898.

Thomas Brooks

Thomas Brooks was another New York cabinetmaker working in Brooklyn. From the 1850s to 1870s, he made furniture in the Gothic, Rococo Revival and Renaissance Revival styles. His rococo pieces are quite distinctive, often with characteristic applied spiral or ropelike borders at the corners (see Fig. 3-10).

At the Crystal Palace Exhibition of New York in 1853, Roux's firm demonstrated its awareness of the latest fashions, exhibiting work in two styles. The company displayed a rosewood rococo armchair and sofa that won critical acclaim. Also displayed were some Renaissance Revival pieces with elaborate carving. The New York Exhibition in 1853 marked the first appearance of the Renaissance Revival style in America, so Roux was a trend-setter.[26] Although he

Fig. 3-9 Sofa, c. 1850, by Alexander Roux featured in A. J. Downing's *The Architecture of Country Houses.* With gracefully curving arms, well-shaped crest rail and apron, and complete with shell carving.

---

26. Diane D. Hauserman, "Alexander Roux and His 'Plain and Artistic Furniture,'" *The Magazine Antiques* 93, no. 2 (February 1968): 213.

27. Ibid., 212.

Charles Baudouine

Also of French descent and with a shop on Broadway in New York City was Charles Baudouine. During the 1850s he employed about 70 people and produced rococo furniture in a rather restrained manner that has more the feeling of 18th-century French furniture than most 19th-century Rococo Revival furniture (see Figs. 3-11, 3-12 and 3-13). Baudouine went to France often and imported furniture. It is difficult to know which pieces he made and which he imported, except through secondary wood analysis.[29]

Fig. 3-10 Rococo Revival rosewood lady's secretary, c. 1860, with satinwood interior, labeled Thomas Brooks, Brooklyn, New York. Mirrored gallery with crest over two mirrored cabinet doors over slant front enclosing writing area. Applied turned pieces. Shaped apron with shell and scroll carving. Cabriole legs. *Courtesy Joan Bogart, Rockville Centre, N.Y.* Dealer estimate: **$3,500–4,800**.

Julius Dessoir

Julius Dessoir also worked in New York City from the 1840s through the 1860s producing pieces in the Rococo Revival style. He exhibited at the New York Crystal Palace Exhibition of 1853. His shop was located with other fine cabinet-makers along the fashionable section of Broadway.[28]

Fig. 3-11 A rare pair of c. 1850 Rococo Revival carved rosewood multiform tables, attributed to Charles Baudouine, New York City. These are designed to be joined together for use as a parlor table, or kept separate as a pair of console or games tables. Each with original baize-lined interior, the apron fitted with a drawer, the carved cabriole "trick" legs extending to receive the fold-over top. Graceful, good proportions. Good condition. 46″ wide × 17″ deep × 30″ high. An identical pair is illustrated in *19th Century American Furniture* by the Metropolitan Museum of Art. *Courtesy Neal Auction Company, New Orleans, Nicolay & Morgan photographers.* **$6,000–9,000**.

---

28. Howe et al, *Herter Brothers*, 64.

29. Eileen and Richard Dubrow, *American Furniture of the 19th Century, 1840–1880* (Atglen, Pennsylvania: Schiffer Publishing, Ltd., 1983), 23.

Fig. 3-12 A single open Baudouine table.

Fig. 3-13 A single folded Baudouine table.

Bembe and Kimbel

In the 1850s the firm of Bembe and Kimbel worked in New York City and also had a shop in Mayenne, France. Kimbel went on to a later partnership with Joseph Cabus with whom he became renowned for Eastlake-inspired furniture.[30]

Leon Marcotte and Ringuet Le Prince

An interesting off-shoot of the Rococo Revival style can be seen in the work of Leon Marcotte and his father-in-law, Ringuet Le Prince, who worked in New York City in the 1860s. They produced furniture that was labeled Louis XVI at the time. It was, in fact, very true to Louis XVI furniture, except in the treatment of color. Marcotte's furniture was ebonized with gilt decoration, whereas in 18th-century France, the furniture would have been decorated and painted a light color—white, gray or pale blue, for example.

The proportions were quite faithful to 18th-century Louis XVI furniture. It was more restrained than most Rococo Revival furniture, with more chaste decorative touches. Although enormously popular in Europe, the Louis XVI Revival style never reached a broad audience in America, where it was not widely produced. It was largely limited to custom-made pieces manufactured in New York City for an elite clientele. Leon Marcotte sold furniture to the likes of John Taylor Johnston, who was the first president of The Metropolitan Museum of Art.[31] Like other revival styles, its arrival in America was due to events in France, where Empress Eugenie, wife of Napoleon III, redecorated in the Louis XVI style. The style was subsequently displayed at the Paris Exposition in 1855 and 1862 London Exhibition.[32]

The firm of Le Prince and Marcotte exemplifies the strong influence of French immigrants on American Victorian furniture. Le Prince had already established his reputation as a leading Paris decorator before he came to New York City in 1849, so his career spanned the old world and the new. After he retired in 1861, the firm continued very successfully under the name Marcotte and Company, both manufacturing and importing, again blurring the boundaries of American Victorian furniture. It can be difficult to determine

30. Ibid., 38.

31. Howe, *Herter Brothers,* 69.

32. Oscar P. Fitzgerald, *Three Centuries of American Furniture* (Englewood Cliffs, N.J.: Prentice-Hall, 1982), 229.

what is American-made and what is French-made.[33]

Philadelphia Makers

Philadelphia was another center for rococo furniture. We have already mentioned George Henkels, who had a thriving business from the 1850s through the 1870s, both as a manufacturer and importer. Other Philadelphia makers include William Allen and his son Joseph, who in the 1830s sold furniture and fine woods. During the 1850s they were known for their fine rococo furniture and custom cabinetwork.[34]

New Orleans Makers

New Orleans, with its large French population, was another important center of rococo furniture. Francois Seignouret worked there from 1811 to 1852, although Prudence Mallard is probably a better-known maker from that area (see Fig. 3-14). Son of a Scottish father and French mother, Mallard worked between 1832 and 1875 and his pieces primarily reflect the Rococo and Renaissance Revivals. He produced and imported furniture from London and Paris. An advertisement from 1857 describes his firm as follows:

Cabinet Maker, Upholsterer, and Dealer in fancy articles. Has always on hand a large

Fig. 3-14 An elegant c. 1850 mahogany Rococo Revival console table, attributed to Prudence Mallard, New Orleans. Serpentine molded top of mahogany (probably marble originally). Conforming frieze is pierce-carved with scrolls and shells. Legs are made up of double C-scrolls with acanthus carving, ending in whorl feet. Molded and shaped stretchers centered by foliate carving. Very graceful overall and close in spirit to the 18th-century French Rococo style, *except* this piece exhibits no asymmetry, the hallmark of the 18th-century Rococo. 60″ long × 19½″ deep × 32″ high. *Private collection.* **$4,500–6,500** as is; **$10,000–15,000** with original marble.

33. Dubrow, 40.
34. Ibid., 13.

stock of highly finished furniture.
Imported and manufactured especially for the
  Southern climate, composed of:
    rich parlor sets, rosewood and mahogany
    bedroom sets, rosewood and mahogany
    library sets, rosewood, mahogany, and

oak—old and modern
dining room sets, rosewood, mahogany,
and oak—old and modern
hall, rosewood, mahogany, and oak—old
and modern[35]

Factory Production

All of the makers discussed up to this point made small quantities of fine furniture for the custom trade. There were also many factories making Rococo Revival furniture. However, little of the factory output has been studied, and the great majority of it is unlabeled, making it difficult to link particular factories with particular pieces. Suffice it to say, the newly growing furniture manufacturers of the era in the major cities of the Eastern Seaboard and the Midwest strove to meet the demand for Rococo Revival pieces. These pieces would not have as much carving or carving of the same quality as that produced by the cabinetmakers for the luxury trade. Factory production captured the curving shapes of the Rococo style and used finger molding and floral carving as embellishments.

Mitchell and Rammelsberg of Cincinnati is one of the few large manufacturing firms that we actually know much about. Founded in 1847, the firm went on to become one of the largest and most successful furniture manufacturers in the Midwest. Cincinnati was one of the Midwestern cities (along with others like Grand Rapids) that had a burgeoning furniture industry and by 1850 had nine steam-powered furniture factories. In that same year, the steam-powered Mitchell and Rammelsberg factory employed 150 workers. For Mitchell and Rammelsberg, the South was an important source of revenue until the Civil War. Then the West proved to be a more lucrative source of income.[36]

Mitchell and Rammelsberg, and other companies like it, soon became a real threat to Eastern manufacturers. One disgruntled author penned this complaint against the competition in 1861:

An immense trade has sprung up in the last few years in a cheap and showy class of furniture, of mongrel design and superficial construction. The location of many dealers in the different cities and towns South and West has increased the demand for this class of good to so great an extent that a number of large steam factories are engaged in this trade exclusively. They make furniture of a showy style, with but little labor on it, and most of that done with the scroll saw and turning-lathe. The dealers both south and west, find this work very profitable, as the showy appearance gives an erroneous idea of value, and purchasers pay more profitable prices for it than they do for good but less pretentious goods. This furniture is easily detected by examination, as it consists mostly of broad, flat surfaces, cut with scroll-saws into all imaginable and unimaginable shapes, and then by a moulding machine the edges are taken off uniformly; this gives it a showy finish. The principle articles thus produced are étagères, or whatnots, fancy tables, hat-racks, bookshelves, music stands, bedsteads, cribs and fancy reception chairs. There is not much of this class of goods that will exist as long as the manufacturer, but will no doubt outlive his reputation as a cabinet-

35. Ibid., 40.

36. Donald C. Peirce, "Mitchell and Rammelsberg: Cincinnati Furniture Manufacturers, 1847–1881," *Winterthur Portfolio* 13 (1979): 217.

maker. This is not to depreciate the value of the goods of any person, but is truthful matter, properly belonging to a work of this kind.[37]

To be fair, we should hear from the other side, provided by a newspaper article in a Cincinnati paper in 1873. The article claimed that Mitchell and Rammelsberg produced "most of the best furniture in the West and South, and not a little in the East." Steam-powered production was defended because "the taste it creates and fosters, the difference in comfort it causes and the almost illimitable employment into which it branches off in every direction is a matter of which any city might boast.... By it, and it alone, the cheapness is the only means of bringing it into thousands of homes to add to their attractions, and thereby . . . to lend its powerful aid in preserving unharmed the mainstay of our national strength, the homelife of our people."[38]

It is the furniture from factories like Mitchell and Rammelsberg that we most often see on the market today. This was the furniture available for those of more modest means. The pieces that we encounter in homes and shops today—with curvaceous lines, simple finger molding, and grapes or a carved flower or two—were made for the middle class. Black walnut was a popular wood; occasionally mahogany was used. The factory pieces were almost totally mass-produced, but not quite. The finger molding was done by hand, as were the carving details. The construction involved dowels and glue for joining parts together—a relatively weak method of joinery. As a result, seating furniture dating from this era often needs to be taken completely apart and reglued.

Later Revivals

Rococo Revival furniture lost popularity during the Civil War, when the Renaissance Revival style became more fashionable. For those in the know, it was becoming passé to have an entire parlor suite of Rococo furniture. However, the occasional rococo chair or table continued to turn up in the more eclectic Victorian parlors of the 1870s and '80s. This revival style had its own revival in the 1920s and again in the 1950s, and these later examples do turn up in antiques malls and estate sales. The best way to distinguish them from 19th-century pieces is to remember that the originals will have more signs of age, better-quality carving, and more generous proportions. Later copies will tend to be taller and thinner and not as graceful as the gorgeous pieces that graced Victorian homes.

---

37. Ibid., 217.
38. Ibid., 219.

One of four walnut side chairs from the same suite as in previous photo. Balloon-shaped back, carved crest rail and horizontal splat, finger-molded and floral-carved apron and legs. Tufted seat. 36″ high. *Private collection.* **$1,800–2,400** the set.

Gentleman's chair from a walnut Rococo Revival parlor suite original to an 1859 home. Balloon-shaped back, finger-molded and carved crest rail, finger-molded arms, cabriole legs and shaped apron. Tufted seat and back. On porcelain casters, 47″ high. *Private collection.* **$650–775**.

Walnut sofa with triple-arching crest rail carved with scrolling acanthus, grapes, fruit and foliage. Appropriately tufted upholstery. 44″ high × 75″ long (From the same set as in previous photo.) *Private collection.* **$1,800–2,400**. A note on suites: While we have typically believed that suites of exactly matching pieces were frequently acquired by Victorians, this house and its furnishings help us to expand our understanding of the period. Two suites—a minor of walnut for the lady's parlor, and a major for the gentleman's parlor—clearly show that some pieces were identical, others similar in style. All of these pieces were original to these rooms in this house, which was built in 1859. We, as dealers and collectors, need to understand this concept as we add to our collections and those of museums and other interpretive settings. Victorians apparently went to the furniture store and created a harmonious suite, with matching upholstery, but not always exactly matching pieces.

Lady's walnut parlor rocker with floral and foliate-carved crest rail, "elbows," plain apron, and appropriately tufted upholstery. 38½″ high. (Not an exact match but from the same suite as in previous photo.) *Private collection.* **$475–650**.

In this same parlor, and original to the 1859 house, is this center table. As is true of this table, the center table generally was not an exact "match" with the parlor seating furniture. This one is walnut, with turtle-shaped marble top. Apron with applied foliate carving. Cabriole legs with rose and scrolling foliate carving. Legs joined by scrolling stretchers centering turned finial. On porcelain casters. 36″ long × 26″ wide × 30½″ high. *Private collection.* **$1,800–2,400**.

Close ups of apron and leg carving. The hand carving found on many Rococo Revival pieces is a real plus in the eyes of today's collectors.

From the same 1859 house, another Rococo Revival parlor suite original to the house (this one for the gentleman's parlor and in rosewood). This suite retains its original upholstery—once a rich red satin, faded with time to a dark brown. The rosewood sofa with triple-arching back topped by finger-molded crest rail and scrolling cabochon crest. Shaped, finger-molded apron and cabriole legs. On white porcelain casters. Tufted upholstery. This suite is really transitional Rococo-Renaissance, the triple-arching form and overall curves being Rococo and the treatment of the crest being more Renaissance. The transitional nature of the suite is fitting to the 1859 date of the house, just about the time when the Renaissance style was overtaking the Rococo in popularity. Sofa is 86″ long × 41½″ high. *Private collection.* **$2,400–3,600**.

Also from the suite, a rosewood gentleman's parlor chair. Again, the shape and finger molding are Rococo in style while the crest is more Renaissance in feeling. *Private collection.* **$900–1,250**.

Also from the suite, one of four upholstered rosewood side chairs. *Private collection.* **$2,400–3,600**, set of four.

Completing the suite is the lady's rosewood parlor rocker, with the same crest treatment. In both parlors in this home the owners chose to substitute the lady's rocker for the lady's chair more commonly found in parlor suites. *Private collection.* **$600–750**.

Rococo Revival walnut parlor suite, c. 1850 (actually a partial double-parlor suite) with two triple-back sofas, two gentlemen's chairs, four wall or side chairs. Tufted upholstery. Pierced and carved crest rails, carved aprons. Front legs on casters. *Courtesy Morton Goldberg Auction Gallery, New Orleans.* **$6,000–9,000.**

Rosewood six-piece Rococo Revival partial double-parlor set, c. 1850–60. With a pair of triple-medallion-back settees (one shown), pair of armchairs, pair of side chairs—all exuberantly carved with high-relief floral and fruited crests and dangling fruit clusters between medallions. Curvate molded frames with out-curved armrests, seats of generous proportions, aprons centered with fruit clusters. Cabriole legs, on casters. Settees are 67″ wide × 24″ deep × 44½″ high. *Courtesy Neal Auction Company, New Orleans, Nicholay & Morgan photographers.* **$10,000–15,000**.

Armchairs and side chairs from the set.

J. and J. W. Meeks "Stanton Hall" pattern laminated rosewood partial parlor suite, consisting of sofa, gentleman's chair, two side chairs and a hall or reception chair. Tufted backs, except for hall chair, which characteristically has an elaborately carved wooden back, meant for looks, not comfort. Pierce-carved crest rails with scrolling acanthus and grape vines within a gadrooned border, centering floral and fruit carving. On casters. *Courtesy Morton Goldberg Auction Gallery, New Orleans.* **$18,000–24,000**.

Transitional c. 1860 Rococo-Renaissance-style walnut gentleman's armchair. With a Renaissance-type crest, though the overall form is Rococo. Well-carved crest and seat rail. 43″ high. *Courtesy the Howard Collection.* **$474–675**.

Rosewood Rococo Revival lady's chair, c. 1850, with tufted back and crest with C-scroll carving. Shaped apron, cabriole legs, whorl feet, on casters. Lady's chairs usually had low arms like these or more truncated "elbows" to allow for voluminous skirts. *Courtesy Crabtree & Company Antiques, Cameron, N.C.* **$600–900**.

Walnut Rococo Revival gentleman's and lady's upholstered chairs, c. 1850. Each with balloon-shaped tufted backs and crest rail with vine and grape carving. Finger-molded frame, arms and apron. On casters. *Courtesy Woodbine Antiques, Oxford, N.C.* **$1,000–1,500** the pair.

Boldly carved walnut Rococo Revival gentleman's chair, c. 1850, with strong C-scrolls, floral and shell carving surmounting and surrounding tufted back. Molded and floral-carved apron. Cabriole front legs. On casters. A strong chair—the product of a fine cabinetmaking shop. 43″ high. *Courtesy the Howard Collection.* **$1,000–1,500.**

Rococo Revival rosewood lady's balloon-back parlor chair, c. 1850. Back crest with floral carving. Molded serpentine apron, cabriole legs, whorl feet, on casters. *Courtesy The Antiques Emporium, Raleigh, N.C.* **$375–475.**

Balloon-back Rococo Revival walnut upholstered lady's chair, c. 1850–60, with finger molding, scrolling "elbow" arms, cabriole front legs on casters. 22″ wide × 39″ high. *Private collection.* **$400–600**.

Walnut Rococo Revival side chair, c. 1860–80. Caned rounded seat, balloon back with incised foilage, pierced scallops and turned spindles. Turned front legs and stretcher. Factory made. 17″ deep × 17″ wide × 33″ high. *Private collection.* **$90–150**.

Walnut Rococo Revival lady's rocker, c. 1860–80. Caned back and seat, scrolling "elbows," turned front legs and stretcher. This probably would have been part of a bedroom suite since the caning and informal nature of the rocker (unless upholstered) were considered more suited to the bedroom. 34" high. *Private collection.* **$175–275**.

Walnut hall chair, c. 1860, with elaborately pierce-carved back with scrolling foliage, flanked by turned stiles topped by finials. Serpentine seat front and apron. Lift lid. Turned front feet. 44" high. *Private collection.* **$375–575**.

Transitional Empire-Rococo sofa, c. 1845–55, of walnut-stained poplar with mahogany flame veneers on crest rail and apron. Triple-section serpentine back. Scrolled apron. Leaf-carved feet, uprights, and crest trims. Old refinished surfaces. 74″ long. *Private collection.* **$750–1,200**.

Walnut transitional Rococo slipper chair, c. 1860, with elaborately pierce-carved keyhole-shaped back-splat flanked by turned stiles and topped by scrolling, foliate-carved crest rail. Rounded seat, with turned legs on rollers. 43″ high. *Courtesy the Howard Collection.* **$375–575**.

Rococo Revival walnut triple-arching sofa, c. 1850. Crest rail with grape and foliate carving. Central portion of tufted back set off in heart-shaped frame. Scrolling, out-flaring arms, shaped and carved apron, cabriole legs, on casters. *Courtesy Flomaton Antique Auction, Flomaton, Ala.* **$1,500–2,400**.

Rococo Revival pierce-carved and laminated rosewood sofa by J. and J. W. Meeks, New York City, c. 1860. With pierced foliate scroll- and grape-carved back above shaped, carved seat rails, raised on cabriole legs. 65½" long. *Sold by Butterfield & Butterfield, Los Angeles.* Part of a five-piece suite that sold for **$7,150**, with an estimate of $8,000–12,000.

Rococo Revival rosewood méridienne, c. 1850, attributed to John Henry Belter. Semi-upholstered seat back framed by large C-scrolls, shell, grape, foliate and floral carving. Shaped and carved apron, carved cabriole legs, on casters. One of a pair, and a rare, desirable form. *Courtesy Witherell Americana Auctions, Elk Grove, California.* Dealer estimate: **$20,000–30,000.**

Rococo Revival laminated rosewood armchair by John Henry Belter, c. 1855. "Arabasket" pattern. Upholstered back surrounded by broadly scrolling pieces that provide the framework for floral, fruit and grape carving. Rose-carved knees, carved apron, cabriole legs with acanthus carving, on casters. *Courtesy Witherell Americana Auctions, Elk Grove, California.* Dealer estimate: **$12,000–15,000.**

A fine c. 1850–65 Rococo Revival laminated rosewood sofa by John Henry Belter, very similar to two others in major museum collections. Three front legs support the undulated, heavily carved seat rail. Arm supports are open. Triple-arching crest rail with masses of floral, fruit and urn carving. *Courtesy Pettigrew Auction Gallery, Colorado Springs.* Sold to a dealer for **$60,500** in 1993. Similar sofas brought $38,385 in England in 1981 and $77,000 from Pettigrew in 1987. Both examples are now in museums.

Laminated rosewood John Henry Belter patent bedstead, branded in several places "J. H. Belter/Patent/August 19, 1856/NY." This is a relatively simple example of Belter's beds, without a pierce-carved crest. Minimal decoration of carved fruit and foliage on the headboard and side rails. The visual impact relies on the beautiful sweeps of curving rosewood veneer. *Courtesy Pettigrew Auction Gallery, Colorado Springs.* Sold for **$17,600** in 1993, though it might have reached into the $25,000–35,000 range.

Laminated rosewood John Henry Belter patent bureau, c. 1860. Branded in several places "J. H. Belter/Patent/New York." With graduated serpentine drawers with scrolling handles, flanked by columns, and the curves continuing into side of the case. Conforming top with molded scrolling standards supporting arched mirror, surmounted by crest with cupids, scrolls and central cabochon. This is the only known example of a Belter patent bureau with figural crest carving, thus increasing its potential value. *Courtesy Pettigrew Auction Gallery, Colorado Springs.* Sold for **$33,000** in 1993, but it might have reached into the $40,000–60,000 range.

Walnut Renaissance Revival sideboard, c. 1860. D-shaped base with two convex doors flanking central door—all with burl panels and Renaissance medallion carving. Three drawers. Marble surface. Top has two long shelves with turned supports. Arching pediment with game and fruit carving flanked by stylized columns. *Courtesy Pettigrew Auction Gallery, Colorado Springs.* **$5,000–7,000.**

Walnut Eastlake cylinder desk, c. 1880. Base with two drawers beside cabinet below one long drawer and cylinder top, all with burl panels. With fitted interior. Two drawers above, with typical Eastlake gallery. Panelled sides and back. 35½" wide × 24" deep × 59¾" high. *Private collection.* **$2,500–3,500.**

Walnut armchair attributed to John Jelliff & Company, c. 1870. Although many cabinetmakers produced furniture with figures on the arms, John Jelliff's usually possessed a higher level of sophistication. Bust carvings on the arm supports. Tufted back surmounted by complex crest featuring portrait medallion, burl panels, roundels, drop finials. Trumpet-turned front legs, on casters. *Courtesy Witherell Americana Auctions, Elk Grove, California.* Dealer estimate: **$2,000–3,000.**

Renaissance Revival maple and rosewood tall chest of drawers, by Herter Brothers, New York City, c. 1870. Cove-molded top incised with scrolling vines over frieze inlaid with repeating palmettes and zigzag border. Five drawers with geometric rosewood escutcheons flanked by rosewood and maple fluted columnar stiles. On stylized bracket feet. 51½" high × 37" wide. *Courtesy Butterfield & Butterfield, Los Angeles.* Sold for **$20,900** in 1991, with an estimate of $8,000–12,000.

Renaissance Revival figured maple and rosewood bedstead, by Herter Brothers, New York City, c. 1870. Architectural headboard with incised and inlaid decoration. Arched, enclosed rosewood-bordered panels. Footboard with similar decoration. This use of highly contrasting woods is an exciting treatment of the Renaissance Revival style, found in the work of the best shops. 8'4" high × 7'5" long × 66" wide. *Courtesy of Butterfield & Butterfield, Los Angeles.* Sold for **$12,100** in 1991, with an estimate of $12,000–18,000.

Pair of Modern Gothic walnut and oak parlor chairs, attributed to Daniel Pabst, design attributed to Frank Furness. Probably for a San Francisco residence, c. 1877. *Courtesy of Butterfield & Butterfield, Los Angeles.* Sold in 1991 for **$1,870,** with an estimate of $3,000–5,000.

Modern Gothic carved walnut and oak settee, attributed to Daniel Pabst, design attributed to Frank Furness, Philadelphia. Probably for a San Francisco residence, c. 1877. 7' long. *Courtesy Butterfield & Butterfield, Los Angeles.* Auction estimate in 1991: **$4,000–6,000** (no sale).

Walnut Rococo Revival triple-back sofa, c. 1850, with finger molding and leaf carving on crest rail, gracefully scrolled apron. Molded cabriole legs, on casters. *Courtesy Woodbine Antiques, Oxford, N.C.* **$1,000–1,500**.

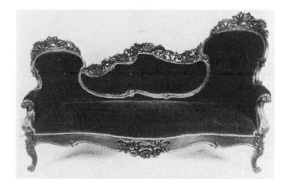

Rococo Revival rosewood asymmetrical sofa, c. 1850—an unusual form that captures the exuberance of this style. Central portion framed in scrolls and topped with elaborate carving. One side of back higher than the other, both topped with scrolls and shell carving. Scrolled arms and apron with asymmetrical carving. Carved cabriole legs. This more accurately mimics true 18th-century Rococo asymmetry than does the typical 19th-century interpretation which uses balance and symmetry throughout. *Courtesy Flomaton Antique Auction, Flomaton, Ala.* **$2,400–3,600**.

Close-up of carving: Another hallmark of Belter furniture is the depth of the carving and the realism achieved by his master carvers. Belter went far beyond most of his contemporaries in the quality of his carving. Also note the layers of lamination visible on the scrolling element below the carving.

Rosewood sofa in John Henry Belter's "Rosalie with Grapes" pattern, c. 1845–65, with triple-arching tufted back. 72½″ long × 40″ high (14″ seat height). *Courtesy the Howard Collection.* **$12,000–18,000**.

Close-up of sofa: Notice how thin the back is. This degree of thinness is possible only with the use of laminations, rather than solid wood. This characteristic of Belter furniture would be virtually impossible to copy today—thus one doesn't have to worry about Belter fakes (only confusion over what patterns are known to have been made by Belter versus the many attributed to him).

Pierce-carved rosewood Belter armchair. New York, c. 1855. *Courtesy Joan Bogart, Rockville Centre, N.Y.* Dealer estimate: **$7,500–10,000**.

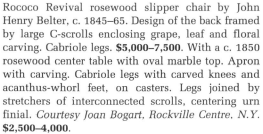

Rococo Revival rosewood slipper chair by John Henry Belter, c. 1845–65. Design of the back framed by large C-scrolls enclosing grape, leaf and floral carving. Cabriole legs. **$5,000–7,500**. With a c. 1850 rosewood center table with oval marble top. Apron with carving. Cabriole legs with carved knees and acanthus-whorl feet, on casters. Legs joined by stretchers of interconnected scrolls, centering urn finial. *Courtesy Joan Bogart, Rockville Centre, N.Y.* **$2,500–4,000**.

Pair of c. 1850–60 Belter recamiers, each with shaped and carved aprons, scrolling legs. Partial backs are tufted and surmounted by heavy scrolls enclosing foliate and grape carving, topped off by foliate-carved crest. These are in wonderful condition and in an unusual pattern, with intricate and delicate pierced carving—thus the dealer estimate of **$25,000–35,000**. *Courtesy Joan Bogart, Rockville Centre, N.Y.*

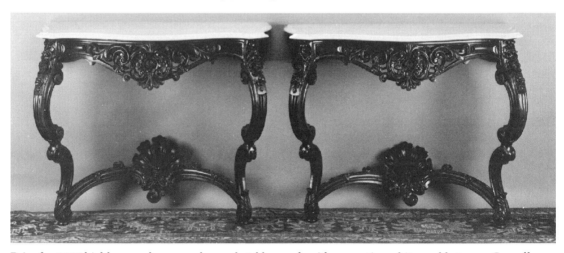

Pair of c. 1850 highly carved rosewood console tables, each with serpentine white marble top on C-scroll supports joined by arched and molded stretchers centering a rocaille-carved shell. Aprons with pierce-carved scrolling designs. These are rare and of wonderful quality. *Courtesy Neal Auction Company, New Orleans, Nicholay & Morgan photographers.* **$8,000–12,000**.

Rococo Revival walnut table, c. 1850–60, with marble turtle-shaped top with S-curved, molded legs joined by stretchers topped in center by an urn finial and drop finial. Simple applied foliate carving below table top. On casters. Original finish. *Courtesy Southampton Antiques, Southampton, Mass.* **$600–900**.

Rococo Revival center table, c. 1850, with turtle-shaped marble top. Molded and shaped apron with applied dropped scrolls. Molded cabriole-type legs (square-sectioned) interrupted by a shelf on which rests a carved dog—the carving is not finely detailed, but rather sketchy. The table legs bump and flare out, creating a line admired during the era. On casters. 33″ long × 20″ wide × 28″ high. *Courtesy Butte's Antiques, Oxford, N.C.* **$800–1,200**.

Rococo Revival laminated rosewood center table, c. 1850, attributed to the J. and J. W. Meeks firm, New York City. Nearly identical to a table at the Munson-Williams Proctor Institute, Utica, N.Y. Oval marble top over scrolling pierce-carved apron. Four beautifully carved cabriole legs are joined by pierce-carved stretchers that pick up motifs in the apron and center a gadrooned urn finial. Whorl feet, on casters. *Courtesy Witherell Americana Auctions, Elk Grove, Calif.* Dealer estimate: **$10,000–15,000**.

Rococo Revival marble-topped console table, c. 1850, with serpentine-shaped top and apron resting on acanthus-carved cabriole legs, shaped stretchers with turned central finial fitted with brass casters. A fairly rare and very desirable form, so long as it was not made from a games table with a replaced top! *Private collection.* **$1,200–1,800**.

Rococo Revival walnut étagère or whatnot, c. 1850–60, with molded and shaped graduated shelves, fret-carved supports and decorations. Original finish. *Southampton Antiques, Southampton, Mass.* **$400–600**.

Rococo Revival rosewood center table, c. 1850–60, with original white marble, elaborately scrolled and pierced apron with mask carving and drop finials. Solid, not laminated. Scrolling, molded X-stretchers with central scrolling carving. Scrolling, acanthus-carved legs. You probably get the idea by now that C-scrolls are the dominant decorative motif of the Rococo Revival style! A handsome, formal table. *Courtesy Joan Bogart, Rockville Centre, N.Y.* Dealer estimate: **$10,000–15,000**.

Rococo Revival walnut étagère, c. 1850–60, with shaped, molded white marble top and conforming lower shelf. Scrolling bracket supports. Elaborately fret-carved pediment featuring urn overflowing with cascading scrolling foliage. Refinished. This is another one of those transitional pieces—Rococo in the scrolling vines of the crest, more Renaissance in feeling in the less-graceful side supports. *Courtesy Southampton Antiques, Southampton, Mass.* **$2,500–3,600**.

Rococo-Renaissance Revival transitional carved rosewood étagère, c. 1850–60, signed by H. Iden, New York. The crest with highly carved grapevine, centered by a mockingbird (detailed and very realistic carving, indicative of the best Victorian work). Mirrored back with three shelves on shaped marble top, on cabriole legs. Apron with another mockingbird eating grapes. This piece has many transitional elements—the volutes, the turned uprights, the lion's head on the side and the repeated use of finials being more Renaissance in style. *Courtesy Neal Auction Company, New Orleans, Nicholay & Morgan photographers.* **$8,000–12,000.**

Detail of crest—spirited carving!

Rococo Revival rosewood secrétaire à abattant (fall-front desk), c. 1850, with fitted interior. Base with foliate-carved cabriole legs and scrolling apron with portrait carving—also found on drawer pulls and crest. Upper section with canted corners and medallion-shaped molding and elaborate foliate carving. Pediment with scrolling foliate carving and portrait below fleur-de-lys. Profoundly influenced by Continental design. *Courtesy Flomaton Antique Auction, Flomaton, Ala.* **$3,500–4,800**.

Rococo Revival carved rosewood cylinder desk/bookcase, c. 1855, attributed to Thomas Brooks. Mirrored upper doors. Cylinder front opens to reveal fitted maple interior with Gothic detailing. Drawer with ovolo molding and scrolling carving. Shaped, molded apron with foliate carving. Cabriole legs with heavy foliate carving on the knees. Whorl feet. Stiles with applied spiral turning. 36½″ wide × 23½″ deep × 61″ high. *Courtesy New Orleans Auction Company, New Orleans.* **$6,000–9,000**.

Rococo Revival rosewood chest of drawers, c. 1850, lined in maple. Serpentine molded white marble top over four serpentine drawers with applied molding and scrolling, plumed escutcheons. No pulls—uses key to open in the European style. Canted corners with applied acanthus carving. Plinth base. Panelled sides and back. Probably made in New York City. 42″ wide × 22¾″ deep × 35½″ high. *Private collection.* **$1,200–1,800.**

Massive c. 1850 Rococo Revival rosewood cylinder desk with applied asymmetrical rococo carving, cabinets flanking panelled kneehole below three over three panelled drawers. Rolltop and stiles with acanthus carving. Upper section with two cabinets identical to lower ones flanking arched cabinet with applied rococo decoration. Scrolling crest centering cabochon and flanked by urn finials. *Courtesy Pettigrew Auction Gallery, Colorado Springs.* **$6,000–9,000.**

Rococo Revival walnut dresser with marble top, c. 1860. Base with four ovolo-molded drawers with wooden foliate handles. Top drawer overhangs. Mirror with beautifully scrolling standards with grapevine entwined, and scalloped upper edges and graceful crest. 44½″ wide × 20″ deep × 81″ high. *Private collection.* **$800–1,200.**

Walnut, flame and crotch walnut veneered Rococo Revival oversized bed, c. 1850. The headboard supported by octagonal standards topped by finials. The headboard itself is a tour de force of graceful rococo carving, complete with scrolling foliage and central cluster of fruit carving, with dangling grape bunches; over three arched panels with flame veneer. Wraparound footboard also with applied fruitful scrolling carving. Beautiful as these beds are, they tend to be so massive they do not suit every house. *Private collection.* **$3,000–5,000**.

Rococo Revival rosewood cylinder-front secretary, c. 1865. Molded cornice topped by urn finials. Two glazed doors enclose tiger maple interior. Cylinder front encloses inlaid interior with racheted writing surface. Below are two panelled cabinet doors with applied fruit carving. Chamfered sides with applied scrolling acanthus and spiral turnings. Panelled sides. Over 9' high with finials. *Courtesy Whitehall at the Villa, Chapel Hill, N.C.* **$8,000–12,000**.

Rosewood Rococo Revival wardrobe or armoire, c. 1850–60, with mirrored door. Scrolled apron, pediment and top of mirror. Fret-carved pediment. Made by Charles Baudouine, New York City. Refinished. *Courtesy Southampton Antiques, Southampton, Mass.* **$6,000–9,000**. Without a known maker, such a wardrobe would bring only **$2,500–4,000**.

A fine Rococo Revival rosewood armoire, signed by J. & J. W. Meeks, with a Vessey Street address (their place of business 1836–1855). Pediment with cabochon, shell, floral and foliate carving. Mirrored door framed by scrolls. Canted corners with scrolling acanthus and floral carving. Drawer above shaped apron. In pristine original condition (always an important factor in deciding value). This is an unusual custom-fitted piece—inside is fitted with a butler's desk with drawer and shelves. *Courtesy Joan Bogart, Rockville Centre, N.Y.* Dealer estimate: **$15,000–20,000**.

4

Renaissance Revival
1860–1880

The Renaissance style overtook the rococo in popularity around the time of the Civil War, with Renaissance remaining immensely popular through the 1870s. The new Renaissance style was inspired in part by Italianate architecture, with its interesting silhouette and arches. It had much in common with the Rococo Revival, including massive proportions, emphasis on formality and richness, and origins in France. But where the Rococo Revival was curvaceous and celebrated the bounty of nature, the Renaissance Revival was based on architectural designs, which gave it a more abstract, monumental, masculine feeling. The Renaissance Revival style was not as graceful as it was massive. Its appeal lay not in balanced curves or naturalistic motifs but in its interesting and imaginative juxtapositions of architectural elements. Arches, ovolo moldings, pediments, plinth bases, cabochons, Renaissance strapwork and scrolls were all arranged in almost endless combinations. Perhaps the exuberance of the Rococo Revival furniture seemed inappropriate for a nation torn by war. Perhaps the more abstract architectural quality and massive scale gave Renaissance Revival furniture a monumental, heroic quality that appealed to the nation at such a difficult time.

Historical Perspective

The Rococo Revival style had an underlying foundation based on C-scrolls and S-scrolls and the graceful curves inspired by 18th-century France—the same sort of unifying theme is not as evident in Renaissance Revival furniture. On the best Rococo Revival pieces the curves provide a graceful underlying structure for the furniture. The same can't really be said of Renaissance Revival, where so many elements compete with each other. The result is an energetic rather than a harmonious feeling. The same aspects that satisfied the huge Victorian appetite for ornament sometimes frustrate the 20th-century aesthetic, which prefers an organic whole. On the other hand, the more abstract, geometric qualities of Renaissance Revival tend to suit those who find the Rococo Revival too frilly by far.

The Renaissance Revival brings together a sometimes confusing melange of styles. The movement originated in mid-19th-century France—and was often referred to as "French Renaissance." The Renaissance Revival style is not at all a copy of furniture of the Renaissance period. True to the Victorian spirit, it is an eclectic borrowing and adapting of architectural motifs not only from the European Renaissance, but also from the baroque and even classical periods. All of these varied elements are mixed together to suit the particular Victorian taste for richness, massive scale, variety, contrast, and visual surprises. Call it what you will, the Victorians clearly loved it.

It may help to think of the movement in two phases. The first phase was a transition from the Rococo Revival, drawing on animal and human figures, flattened arches, and ovolo molding, with walnut as the most prominent wood. Typical of this early phase is the corner cabinet, shown in Fig. 4-1, with simple applied arched and ovolo molding, carved wood fruit handles and panelled doors and sides. A common chair might have finger molding, as on rococo chairs, and a cabochon crest. As with the rococo style, one finds lots of naturalistic carving featuring fruit and sometimes animals. Fruit-carved handles are ubiquitous on these pieces. For the most part, these are conservative pieces with rela-

Fig. 4-1 Renaissance Revival carved walnut curved-front marble top corner cabinet, c. 1860. Pie-shaped white marble top over a drawer and pair of cabinet doors with arched molding and carved fruit motifs. 51″ wide × 36″ deep × 39″ high. *Courtesy Neal Auction Company, New Orleans, Nicolay & Morgan photographers.* **$1,000–1,500.**

tively simple decoration. This style continued to be produced alongside the later phase and was sold to a more conservative segment of the market.

Néo-Grec

The later phase of the style is more assertive, moving away from naturalistic carving and becoming more abstract. The style and the name, Néo-Grec, are French in origin. Like the other Victorian styles, this one made its first appearance at the great international exhibitions. The Néo-Grec style was first displayed by the French at the 1862 London Exhibition and again at the Paris Exposition of 1867. In America the style was sometimes called Modern Greek, New Greek, New Grecian or, by the French label, Néo-Grec. Today this later phase is often simply called "Renaissance Revival," which is not incorrect. However, to be more specific, we will call it Néo-Grec.

In general, the naturalistic carving found in the earlier phase is replaced by architectural motifs and motifs borrowed from Greece, Rome and sometimes Egypt. While some naturalistic ornament is used, it is more stylized. The overall appearance is more geometrical, two-dimensional, flatter—in short, more abstract. The Néo-Grec style is highly architectural, with classical entablatures, complex pediments, medallions, columns, plinth bases, roundels, finials, drops, cabochons, palmettes and urns as hallmarks (see Fig. 4-2). Extra contrast is sometimes achieved through the use of dark and light woods.

The chief characteristics of Néo-Grec furniture are abrupt contrast and aggres-

Fig. 4-2 Richly ornamented cabinet, c. 1876, with marquetry panels and Néo-Grec detail—probably the most lavish form of furniture to appear in Victorian America. By Kimbel and Cabus, New York City. The firm's 1876 design book, now in the Cooper Hewitt Museum, gives us an historic and important overview of their work; this cabinet is #4 in the book, and it originally sold for $200. [Art and Antiques, ed. *Nineteenth Century Furniture: Innovation and Reform* (New York: Billboard Publications, 1982), 62.] Its purpose was purely aesthetic—to display an important piece of sculpture. Rosewood and ebonized wood, with extensive marquetry, porcelain plaques and gilt-incised decoration. *Courtesy Witherell Americana Auctions, Elk Grove, Calif.* Dealer estimate: **$15,000–25,000**.

sive, mannered design. This design treatment comes across in terms of motifs that are overdone, elongated or exaggerated—treated in a manner that brings attention to the individual motif and creates the effect of competing parts rather than an organic whole. The overall result is often bizarre composition featuring jagged outlines.[1]

The triple-back or tripartite sofas typical of both the general Renaissance Revival style and especially the Néo-Grec style provide a good example of the aesthetic. Obviously strongly divided, the parts create tension in the overall design, which is not allowed to resolve as it would in furniture of a more classical mode. When we admire this furniture, it becomes clear what the Victorians loved—novelty, strong contrasts and visual excitement. Subtlety or simplicity was not for them![2]

By the 1870s, factories were also producing this visually exciting style. In the factory setting, machine processes dictated a flatter style; high-relief carving, which had to be done by hand, was omitted on all but the most expensive pieces. Factory pieces got their Néo-Grec flare from panels of burl walnut contrasted with incised lines (sometimes with gilt), and applied roundels, turned drop finials, palmettes and complex pediments.[3] For the less expensive items, this was a popular look for small pieces like wall pockets (see Fig. 4-3), hanging cabinets, display easels, small tables, urn stands, and sewing stands. The sharp contrasts, spiky turnings, and protruding elements all create an agitated effect. It was an exciting look that seems rather eccentric to the 20th-century eye.

---

1. Kenneth L. Ames, "What is the Néo-Grec?," *Nineteenth Century* 2, no. 2 (Summer 1976): 14.

2. Kenneth L. Ames, "Grand Rapids Furniture at the Time of the Centennial," *Winterthur Portfolio* 10 (1975): 47–49.

3. Ames, "What is the Néo-Grec?" 18.

Fig. 4-3 Néo-Grec walnut wall pocket, c. 1870–80, with medallion of cherubs playing musical instruments. One of its uses would have been to hold sheet music. The "pocket" is secured by a chain held by a lion's head. With gilt-incised decoration, ebonized accents, applied roundels, broken pediment with stylized palmette and scrolls or plumes. 30″ high × 18″ wide. *Private collection.* **$500–750.**

Egyptian Revival

An interesting but limited subset of the Renaissance style was the Egyptian Revival. The fad for Egyptian things came to America by way of Napoleon's discoveries in Egypt in the late 18th century. A massive tome was published with the findings, including an exhaustive catalog of Egyptian decorative motifs. During the Napoleonic era, French furniture did not escape the Egyptian influence. From the 1860s through the 1880s the craze made its way to America, but only in the work of a few custom cabinetmaking shops in New York like Pottier and Stymus, Alexander Roux, and Leon Marcotte. The number of pieces is fairly small, but they are unmistakable, bearing motifs such as anthemion, palmettes, Egyptian animals, scarabs, the eastern star, spirals, zigzags, and bold colors.[4] These motifs are also incorporated onto Eastlake-type forms, as seen in some of the photographs in Chapter 6.

Mechanization

All of this decorative extravagance was made possible by increasing mechanization at the burgeoning factories of the period. By the 1870s the large Midwestern factories in places like Grand Rapids were able to mass-produce almost all of the decorative elements found on Renaissance Revival pieces—roundels; turned ornaments like finials, drops, urns or turned legs; panelling; molding; incised

4. Art and Antiques, ed., *Nineteenth Century Furniture: Innovation, Revival and Reform* (New York: Billboard Publications, 1982), 44–46.

decoration. Only high-relief carving still had to be done by hand. In short, the factories were perfectly suited to produce this furniture which satisfied the taste for grandeur and richness without being out of reach economically. Factories were well suited to manufacturing a range of grades—adding more ornament and using more expensive materials for the higher lines. Steam-powered woodworking machines played a significant role in producing the average factory suite of Renaissance Revival furniture; only the most expensive pieces would be accented with high-relief carving done by hand. The Rococo Revival, with its extraordinary naturalistic carving, generally required more handwork.

The comparative ease of producing Renaissance Revival styles may have led to its greater popularity. George W. Gay, partner in Berkey and Gay, one of Grand Rapids's largest furniture manufacturers, made this comment on the Renaissance Revival style: "Manufacturers looked for a fashion in which they could use their facilities to the best advantage, and at the same time retain the attractiveness of their earlier work. This they found in the Renaissance, which for a number of years superseded all other styles in the best class of furniture."[5] In fact, this kind of furniture owes its existence to mechanized factories; its widespread popularity would never have been possible in an age of cabinetmakers working by hand. In this way, the Renaissance Revival style epitomizes the Victorian age with its combined love of richness and worship of technological progress.

After the war, furniture production expanded dramatically, especially in the new Midwestern factories. Between 1860 and 1870 the furniture industry as a whole more than doubled in size, with much of the growth occurring in the new factories in the Midwest—Cincinnati and Cleveland, Ohio; Indianapolis, Indiana; and, especially, Grand Rapids, Michigan.[6] These new furniture centers gained the advantage over more established factories on the Eastern Seaboard because, from the start, they were designed and built to incorporate the latest new machinery. This situation made furniture available to a broader range of the population, and it drove smaller operations out of business.

The number of factories producing Renaissance Revival furniture must have been legion. However, at the present time, not much is known about which factories made which pieces. Most of their production cannot be distinguished today due to lack of documentation. Also, factories all over the country tended to use the same woodworking machines, which contributed to a similarity in design. We do know that the large steam-powered factories in Grand Rapids, Michigan, were very active during the 1870s mass-producing Renaissance pieces and shipping them all over the country. Berkey and Gay, Phoenix Furniture Company and Nelson, Matter and Company all had large new factories by the early 1870s and were poised to supply the country with their goods. They had new buildings designed for optimum use with the latest equipment.[7]

These three Grand Rapids companies took full advantage of the Centennial Exhibition in 1876, where they displayed eye-catching suites in the Renaissance style. All three won awards. Nelson, Matter and Company displayed a massive beadstead and dresser in the Renaissance style with almost life-sized statues of the founding fathers. For all three companies,

5. Ames, "Grand Rapids Furniture," 34.

6. Mary Jean Smith Madigan, "The Influence of Charles Locke Eastlake on American Furniture Manufacture, 1870–90," Winterthur Portfolio 10 (1975):5.

7. Ames, "Grand Rapids Furniture," 28–31.

these were clearly exhibition pieces showing their finest materials, designs and execution—the kinds of pieces that made reputations. Of course, each produced great quantities of low-end goods as well, many of which we find on the market today. After the Centennial, several Grand Rapids firms expanded their markets with new showrooms in New York City. They further increased their market share with an important innovation—the semiannual furniture market, attended by buyers from all around the country.

By 1880 these factories had grown tremendously. Berkey and Gay employed 400 people, with product valued at $525,000; Phoenix had 520 workers and goods worth $514,000; Nelson, Matter employed 380 and valued its production at $315,000.[8] Each company had its own staff of designers to create designs to suit popular taste. A large part of the trade consisted of suites for the bedroom and parlor.[9]

Grand Rapids was, of course, not the only manufacturing center. Another important site was Cincinnati, Ohio, home of Mitchell and Rammelsberg, which was one of the largest manufacturers off the East Coast. They shipped their Renaissance Revival furniture to the South and other parts of the country. Their styles were sometimes more flamboyant while those from Eastern manufacturers were more conservative.

These large factories provided competition that threatened the livelihood of many a small cabinetmaker. Smaller firms might not be able to match the low prices of factories, but they could claim better quality. Even during the Victorian era, the attitudes towards mechanization were mixed, and smaller firms could get an edge by appealing to these misgivings. Some companies' advertisements claimed

the advantages of both—the latest, most progressive machines and also a staff of skilled artisans. Others emphasized that all the work was done by hand, an attempt to distance themselves from what they would have called the shoddy work of the large new factories. Smaller firms had to appeal to a different market to stay in business at all, offering pieces that were made with time-tested construction and more handwork, appropriate for a segment of the monied population. Of course, it can be difficult to interpret advertising—we expect exaggeration—but it is clear that the advertisers were in touch with the public's mixed feelings about advancing technology.

Many smaller firms drew attention to the fact that they were not steam-run, and emphasized that much of the work was still done by hand. An older firm in Baltimore described itself thus, ". . . the mammoth stock of goods elegant in design, style, and finish presents one of the most complete and perfect displays of *hand-made* Furniture in the city . . . everything in the line of first-class Fine Cabinet Furniture for parlor, chamber and office use is always to be found in stock."[10]

Furniture historians are just beginning to explore the role of mechanization in the 19th-century furniture trade. It is difficult to say with certainty when specific machines would have been used and in what settings. The process of mechanization was constantly evolving and differed depending on the size of the shop.

The furniture industry had several levels. There were large factories which used powered machinery as much as possible for the bulk of their furniture, and perhaps used hand work on a limited basis for production of high-end pieces. There were also small cabinetmaking shops, perhaps making limited use of

---

8. Ibid., 32.

9. Ibid., 30–32.

10. Gregory R. Weidman, *Furniture in Maryland, 1740–1940* (Baltimore: Maryland Historical Society, 1984): 207.

steam-powered machinery but also keeping alive the tradition of hand work. These small firms had several options open to them. They could buy machines—steam-powered, horse-powered or foot-powered—that they could use regularly and could afford. They could also contract out to firms specializing in one aspect of the trade. For example, mill houses were equipped with circular saws and planing machines to cut boards, and they often had other machines as well—lathes, fret saws, shapers and molders to provide shaped pieces, turned pieces, roundels, etc. The third level of mechanization was exemplified by the fine cabinetmaking firms in major cities which employed many workers. They produced custom-designed furniture using quality construction methods and also used steam-powered machinery when it was cost-effective but not when it compromised the quality of the decoration.

Fine cabinetmaking firms like Herter Brothers used high-quality woods and panelled construction, and employed artisans who were skilled in carving and gilding. Obviously, there were some steps that simply had to be completed by hand. Of course, this was furniture for the luxury trade, made for wealthy clients like railroad magnates and industrialists, and today this furniture is among the most collectible of the Victorian era. Clearly, the quick dismissal of Victorian furniture on the grounds that it was all mass produced using shoddy construction techniques is neither fair nor accurate.

Period reporting of exhibits at the Centennial adds to our understanding of how new woodworking technologies were used. As a showcase for the nation's industrial strength, the Centennial had prominent displays of the latest devices. The exhibit of J. A. Fay & Company's woodworking machinery was featured in an 1876 issue of *Scientific American,* which pictured and described the various machines (see Fig. 4-4). There were machines for planing, tongue and groove (for

Fig. 4-4 The exhibit of A. J. Fay & Company's woodworking machinery at the Centennial. From *Scientific American,* November 1876.

flooring), machines for molding the edges of panels, incising, making tenons, band saws (which could cut curving outlines), rip saws and fret or scroll saws that did not run off the edge of the stock and thus could cut inside the outlines.

A few years later, an 1880 issue of *Scientific American* (see Fig. 4-5) again featured woodworking machines, this time in use at the factory of M. & H. Schrinkeisen in New York City where about 200 parlor suites in any one design could be produced at one time. There were machines for planing, turning, sanding, a jointer that smoothed the joints between boards, band saws and fret or scroll saws, a variety molder to do all sorts of moldings. But we should notice that not all of the work could be accomplished with machines. A spindle carver is pictured, and the magazine's description is

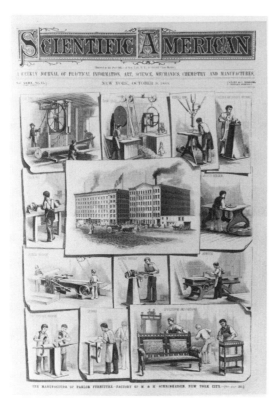

Fig. 4-5 Woodworking machinery featured in an October 1880 issue of *Scientific American.*

(including multiple carvers or direct-copying carvers) were so complex and expensive that they were only economical in a large mass-production setting. A machine that undertook a particularly complex task could necessitate frequent changes of settings, changes of cutting tools, etc. The complexity made this type of machine practical only for a large factory making thousands of copies. These factories would also require skilled workers who knew how to operate and fix these machines. The cost of upkeep—new cutting knives, new parts—had to be considered. The cost of steam or coal or electric power had to be taken into consideration when calculating the true cost of this kind of production.[12]

Of all the carving machines, the spindle carver pictured in *Scientific American* came closest to replicating hand carving. But even it was not capable of the depth, undercutting and complexity of high-relief, three-dimensional hand carving. This kind of carving simply could not be done by machines. New technologies could not always *replicate* work done by hand, and when the difference between machine work and hand work was obvious to the eye, hand work would take precedence on high-quality furniture.

As we keep in mind the range of quality and degrees of mechanization in late 19th-century furniture, it is undeniable that a great deal of it was mass produced and inexpensive. The large factories in the Midwest and in major Eastern cities aimed to produce affordable furniture for an expanding population. Many factories produced goods with an eye to shipping by boat or railroad across the country or abroad. In this case, pieces were designed especially for crating and easy assembly upon arrival. Goods to be shipped were sometimes left unfinished, as the finish could be damaged by the extreme condi-

instructive. The wood was hand held against the cutting knives.

In this way the machine may be adjusted to do almost any kind of carving desired, but it is found more economical in practice to do a large proportion of the carving by hand, rather than fit up the knives and patterns for the machine for all the new and elaborate designs in carving which are always being introduced. . . . The carving by hand, of which a view is given in one of our illustrations, forms a very important part of the work done at the establishment, at which thirty to forty hands are kept regularly employed.[11]

This comment on the spindle carver illustrates several important points about emerging technologies. Some machines

11. *Scientific American* (October 6, 1880): 229.

12. Michael J. Ettema, "Technological Innovation and Design Economics in Furniture Manufacture," *Winterthur Portfolio* 16, nos. 2/3 (Summer/Autumn 1981): 198.

tions of long storage. Pieces could easily be finished or painted by the retailer who ordered the goods or even by the final purchaser. This kind of furniture was absolutely vital to new settlers on the Western frontier and other remote areas of the country.

Room Settings and Furniture Forms

The Hall

In Victorian America, one did not simply place furniture according to personal whim. Furniture was felt to have an important symbolic purpose, and the Renaissance Revival style was used to make a grand, imposing effect in formal areas of the home.

One often found Renaissance Revival–style furniture in halls, the area of the home where first impressions were vital. In an era when visiting was an important activity played out in subtle social rituals, the hall was a formal area that first conveyed the status of the household. In affluent households, the most prominent piece of furniture was usually the hallstand, a Victorian invention that was a mark of status and served social customs (see Fig. 4-6). It was a huge piece of furniture—often six to ten feet tall. Its bulk alone gave it importance and formality. It usually consisted of a mirror, often framed in undulating curves and studded with hooks or knobs for hats and coats. Below the mirror might be a stand with a marble top and drawer. It would be flanked by holders for walking sticks and umbrellas, with drip pans below. Elaborate hallstands had cast-metal drip pans, the best might even have marble, while cheaper models made do with tin.

The hallstand provided a formal space for visitors to leave their personal cards with subtle clues as to their feelings towards you, their status and yours. Calling cards were part of an intricate social ritual for paying respects by visiting in person or by leaving one's card. Social calling was an important and time-consuming duty of the well-to-do wife. However, the goal could also be achieved by leaving a card and not having a face-to-face visit. The person being visited could be "not at home" (upstairs, out of sight and not wanting to be bothered), and one could simply leave a card and still do

Fig. 4-6 Walnut Renaissance Revival hallstand, c. 1860, with sturdy hooks, applied veneer panels and roundels, pediment top crowned with high-relief-carved crest. Arched mirror. Base with marble-topped table with freize drawer, strongly turned legs, cast iron drip pans. Approximately 9′ high. *Private collection.* **$1,800–2,400.**

one's duty without breaking a single rule of etiquette. We might consider this arrangement highly artificial, but at least it allowed social ties to be maintained without social exhaustion. Orderly social connections were a mainstay of Victorian society, and the hallstand was a prop for this vital activity. As such, it needed to make a commanding presence through the use of luxurious materials like mirrors and burl veneers, and boasting, extravagant decoration.

The Dining Room

The dining room afforded another formal setting for much Renaissance Revival furniture. For the middle class, who now bought vast quantities of furniture, a room set apart just for dining was a relatively new concept. During most of the 18th century there had been no separate room for dining, except in the grand homes of the wealthy. A drop-leaf table in the living room sufficed for a dining table. By the mid-19th century, prosperous middle class homes had a separate dining room, generally outfitted in the Renaissance Revival style. Pedestal tables had replaced the drop-leaf table for the most part. By about 1850, extension pedestal tables became fashionable, and this massive form remained the most prevalent dining table throughout the second half of the century.

The Victorians considered the dining room to be masculine. This was, of course, a carryover from the 18th century, when women retired to the drawing room (or with-drawing room) after dinner, and the men drank, smoked and conversed at the dining table. Many 18th-century and early 19th-century sideboards of the superior quality indicative of wealthy owners have a small side compartment that, surprisingly enough, contained the urinals for the men to use once the ladies departed and drinking became more robust. Screens were also kept in dining rooms for more substantial events.

In Victorian America this sort of behavior would never have been allowed. The dining room provided an opportunity to display the family's wealth—and display it they did. The massive Renaissance Revival sideboards, with their extravagant carving, were outward signs of the family's wealth and status (see Fig. 4-7). They were not particularly functional, with little storage space considering their bulk. Such a sideboard was primarily a display

Fig. 4-7 Massive oak Renaissance Revival sideboard, c. 1865. A tour de force of high-relief carving and just one step down from the fantastic sideboards on display at the international exhibitions. With intricately shaped base featuring three curved doors, each with lavish carvings of game, fish, vegetables and fruit. Pilasters between the doors also boast food carvings, including heads of cows. Oak serving surface (not marble). Top with two shelves and back with bosses framed by diamonds below carving of birds and fruit in a domed pediment. Surmounted by a gadrooned urn holding masses of fruit and vegetables. The sides are bordered by mythical beasts with web feet and griffin heads. 84″ wide × 9′4″ high. *Courtesy Butte's Antiques, Oxford, N.C.* Dealer's estimate: **$20,000–35,000.**

piece that made a strong symbolic and aesthetic statement. As with much high-style Victorian furniture, its visual qualities were more important than its functional ones.

At the exhibitions that shaped design evolution in the second half of the century, sideboards played an important role, representing the best and very height of carving and magnificence a country could produce. At the Crystal Palace Exhibition in London in 1851, France made an aggressive statement about its dominance in the decorative arts when it displayed an important, massive Renaissance Revival sideboard absolutely covered with high-relief naturalistic carving of foodstuffs and hunting motifs. At the 1853 New York International Exhibition, similar sideboards were on display. Steeped in motifs of the hunt, these sideboards help us understand the Victorian concept of the dining room as a masculine place. The connection between food, hunting, and death was not only made but also celebrated on these massive sideboards. Of course, these exhibition pieces were impossible to reproduce for ordinary homes. However, affluent households soon possessed similar models that copied the spirit, if not every detail, of the exhibition pieces.

The basic form was as follows: a base of four units, each with a door (the center doors being flat, the side doors convex)—all with carving and often with burl panels and molding framing the carving. Above the doors were four conforming drawers, similarly decorated with panelling and molding. The base was topped by a flat marble surface, which was divided into three sections (center and two sides) by the graduated shelves resting on it. There was often a mirrored backing for the shelves. The very top of the piece boasted a magnificent crest, usually highlighting the bounties of the hunt.[13]

In affluent Victorian homes, sideboards provided a dramatic backdrop for the important family rituals, the aim of which were to solidify bonds of community. Dining was far more than simple sustenance—it was a complex activity for the Victorians, full of significance. Above all, dining was meant to show how far man had advanced from the beast. These highly refined behaviors expressed the Victorian notion of "progress," dominance over nature and even suppression of man's own animal or bestial tendencies. For the well-to-do, seated in their opulently furnished dining rooms, the very act of eating involved using an extraordinary number of different utensils, each with a particular purpose. By the end of the century, the Victorian innovation of matching silverware meant sets of as many as 131 different pieces![14]

It is fascinating to note that even in such a setting, the violence of nature was a prominent theme and in fact, was depicted not only on sideboards but also in other 19th-century arts—for example, in the paintings of Eugene Delacroix and the bronze sculptures of Antoine Louis Barye. Romantic images glorified man's domination over nature—in savage displays of power and strength, in which man was always victorious. It seems appropriate that the same era produced Charles Darwin's *On the Origin of Species* (1859).[15]

Being such forceful pieces, these sideboards have often aroused strong feelings, not all of them positive. Reform writers in the 1870s singled them out for particular scorn. One writer described them thus: "Monsters besmeared with stain and varnish, grin at you from every point, and you cannot even open a drawer on a cupboard

13. Kenneth L. Ames, *Death in the Dining Room and Other Tales of Victorian Culture* (Philadelphia: Temple University Press, 1992), 67.

14. Kathryn Grover, editor, *Dining in America, 1850–1900* (Amherst: University of Massachusetts Press, 1987), 181.

15. Ames, *Death in the Dining Room,* 68.

without having your feelings outraged by coming into contact with the legs or wings of a dead bird or some other ghastly trophy of man's love of slaughter, which frequently take the place of an ordinary handle."[16]

The Parlor

In contrast to the dining room, the parlor was relatively untouched by violence and controversy. The basic forms of furniture continued unchanged from the Rococo Revival era, with only the adoption of Renaissance Revival shapes and motifs. The seven-piece parlor suite remained a middle-class convention. The sofa, gentleman's and lady's chairs and several wall or side chairs were still grouped in an orderly fashion around a marble-topped center table. Finer parlor suites often feature portrait carving or bronze medallions with busts. Whereas rococo chairs have round or oval backs, those on Renaissance Revival chairs are rectangular but flare out at the top. This is a nice effect that adds to the energetic angularity of Renaissance Revival designs.

The étagère also remained popular in the parlor as a focal point for displaying porcelains and other *objets d'art* (see Fig. 4-8). The Renaissance Revival étagerès often have irregularly cutout backs with molded edges (some holding mirrors). These rather eccentric shapes create an overall unpredictable, undulating silhouette—a marked departure from the graceful, scrolling outlines of the Rococo Revival style. These irregular shapes are not a revival of any historical style—they are purely the product of a lively Victorian imagination, aided by steam-powered fret saws that could cut out almost any curve.

Renaissance Revival parlor tables and side tables eschew the obvious, functional form of a square top with a leg at each corner. This form held little interest for the Victorians, who seemed to prefer the sometimes awkward (and structurally weaker) form of a top supported by four legs clustered in the center and curving in unexpected, highly unusual ways (see Fig. 4-9). One might look at these tables and discover an underlying rule: the more

Fig. 4-8 Renaissance Revival faux-bois rosewood étagère, probably New York, c. 1860. Cartouche centered by clusters of nuts and leaves flanked by lavish foliate and S-scroll embellishments. Central mirror flanked by six shelves backed by interestingly shaped mirrored and cutout areas. Central marble top over drawer over shaped-apron base. The piece with the undulating, exciting silhouette favored by the Victorians. 90″ high × 49″ wide × 22″ deep. *Courtesy New Orleans Auction Company.* **$4,000–6,000.**

---

16. Rhoda and Agnes Garrett, *Suggestions for House Decoration in Painting, Woodwork, and Furniture* (Philadelphia: Porter & Coates, 1877), 49. Cited in Martha Crabill McClaugherty, "Household Art: Creating the Artistic Home, 1868–1893," *Winterthur Portfolio* 18, no. 1 (Spring 1983): 18.

Fig. 4-9 Renaissance Revival walnut and gilt-incised decorated fern stand, c. 1860. Molded circular top framing inset variegated rust marble raised on central column flanked by three fluted columns extending to splayed fluted legs. With applied roundels and finials. 20″ wide × 18″ deep × 30½″ high. *Neal Auction Company, New Orleans, Nicolay & Morgan photographers.* **$600–900**.

bizarre, the better. Obviously, visual surprises, complexity and richness were hallmarks of the Victorian aesthetic. Decorative effect often won out over sound principles of construction.

Atop any interesting base rested a slab of elegant marble. It offered contrast to the dark wood base, and it added richness and formality to the piece. Although it was far from practical—it was heavy, expensive, and breakable—everyone insisted on it. It, too, was an important part of the Victorian aesthetic which valued the use of contrasting materials and the effect of luxury. Marble was used extensively—on most tables (except for forms like flip-top games tables), for dressers and hallstands. Only on the cheapest grades was wood substituted for marble.

The Bedroom

Marble and massive furniture were also found in the bedroom, where beds and dressers were commonly over eight feet high. Suites in the early phase of the Renaissance style have applied fruit carving and arched headboards and footboards with ovolo molding. These are monumental pieces and the more architecturally styled beds, which often evoke church facades, have great dignity and a commanding presence.

Most of the beds from this period had a high headboard joined by straight side rails to a similarly decorated lower footboard. Slats supported the mattress. Canopy beds were uncommon. The more expensive the bed, the finer the wood and the more decoration, including hand carving. The companion dressers were equally impressive, with similar decoration—including veneer panels and applied carving. The form was usually three drawers below a marble surface flanked by glove boxes and supporting a tall mirror. Finer dressers with larger mirrors, were called cheval dressers or dressing cases. Because this type of dresser usually had less drawer space, a suite might also include a wardrobe for extra storage. Suites might also contain a gentleman's dresser (a tall chest with no mirror), a marble-topped washstand and night tables, as well as a shaving stand and bootjack for the gentleman. These pieces did not always match, strictly speaking, but they did make use of related motifs and materials. They were not clones but cousins.

Production of bedsteads lent itself easily to mechanization. Except for high-relief applied carving on crests, practically everything else could be done by steam-powered machines. The carving, of course, might be contracted out to a carving firm or done by carvers in-house. The construction techniques on case pieces for bedroom suites was more complicated and joinery was not entirely done by machines.

Cabinetmaking Firms

Kimbel and Cabus

Although the vast majority of Renaissance Revival furniture that we see today was made by the large factories and is rarely labeled, there were also a number of well-known highly respected firms working in the style. Kimbel and Cabus made some of the finest Néo-Grec furniture, particularly the monumental cabinets with porcelain plaques and marquetry panels, which were used as a base for sculpture (see Fig. 4-2 on page 71). Their work is characterized by the use of expensive materials like porcelain plaques (usually from France), ormolu mounts, gold-leaf accents, marquetry and exotic woods like ebony. Kimbel and Cabus operated in New York City from 1863 to 1882. Anthony Kimbel, a designer, had previously worked with Anthony Bembe and had a factory and clients in France as well as in America. Kimbel had also worked with Charles Baudouine, another maker of very fine French-style furniture. Joseph Cabus, a cabinetmaker, had worked with Alexander Roux. Obviously, Kimbel and Cabus brought to their partnership experience with some of the finest furniture makers of the period.[17]

Fig. 4-10 Renaissance Revival tripartite sofa by John Jelliff, Newark, c. 1865. Walnut, reupholstered. With busts and carved portrait medallions. Strongly turned legs, drops on apron, drop finials on sofa back. Imposing carved crest rail. *Courtesy Southampton Antiques, Southampton, Mass.* **$4,000–6,000.**

17. Art and Antiques, ed., 60–63.

John Jelliff

Another firm that produced distinctive Renaissance Revival work was John Jelliff & Company of Newark, New Jersey. At age 14, Jelliff had been apprenticed to a carver for a brief period, and his earliest training must have influenced him greatly as his designs feature strong carvings of heads and busts (see Fig. 4-10). The shop he set up in Newark, in 1843 is known to have produced pieces in several revival styles—Gothic, Elizabethan, Rococo and Renaissance. He was forced to retire in 1860 due to illness, but he continued to advise the firm. The company maintained the Jelliff name until 1890, when it was changed to Henry W. Miller, Successor to John Jelliff & Company. Jelliff died in 1893, and the business disbanded in 1901 after Miller's death.[18]

An 1874 survey of manufacturers tells us that the Jelliff factory had 40,000 square feet of floor space, employed 45 men and did an annual business of $100,000. The firm produced fine custom work, with half of the sales outside of Newark, in such places as New York City, elsewhere in New Jersey, Washington, Richmond, and further south. The firm produced furniture—from the medium grades to the finest, most expensive quality—for the parlor, dining room, library and bedroom, and for commercial offices. Jelliff is best known for his Renaissance Revival parlor sets which displayed strongly carved classical busts on the crests and arm terminals. True to his early training, his chief decoration was carving. He almost never used inlay and rarely paint, although his incised lines were often touched with gold.[19]

Alexander Roux

Alexander Roux worked in the French styles, both manufacturing and importing pieces. Roux worked in New York City from 1837 to 1881, with his firm continuing under a son until 1898. He maintained close contact with his brother, who was a maker of fine furniture in Paris.[20]

His exhibit at the 1853 Crystal Palace Exhibition in New York City proved to be on the cutting edge of fashion. In response to the fabulous Renaissance sideboards made by the French, he exhibited an ornate black walnut sideboard with game, fish and other foodstuffs. He also made other Renaissance pieces in the 1850s, along with pieces that have an Elizabethan look, characterized by vigorously spiral-turned legs and pierce-carved panels.

Thomas Brooks

Cabinetmaker Thomas Brooks (1811–1887) was also involved with the 1853 New York Exhibition. His execution of a design by Gustave Herter for a richly carved rosewood Renaissance étagère won a bronze medal.[21] Brooks worked in Brooklyn, New York, between 1850 and 1870, making fine pieces styled according to Gothic, Rococo and Renaissance Revivals.

George Hunzinger

George Hunzinger's furniture can certainly be called Renaissance in style, but because his designs were so distinctive and incorporate his own patented innovations, his work is discussed in Chapter 5.

---

18. J. Stewart Johnson, "John Jelliff, Cabinetmaker," *The Magazine Antiques,* 206 (August 1972): 256.

19. Ibid., 256–260.

20. Katherine S. Howe et al. *Herter Brothers: Furniture and Interiors for a Gilded Aged* (New York: Harry N. Abrams, 1994), 66.

21. Howe et al, *Herter Brothers,* 67.

Herter Brothers

Herter Brothers of New York City is better known for furniture in the Eastlake or Aesthetic movement style (see Chapter 6), but the company produced other styles as well. Gustave and Christian Herter were German immigrants whose furniture and decorating firm became the most prestigious of the 1870s. They were in touch with design trends in Europe and England and created their own luxurious interpretations. Their Renaissance Revival pieces, custom made for well-to-do clients around the country in the 1860s and early '70s, featured robust hand carving. Their carefully made furniture used panelled construction and fine woods and almost always demonstrates an eye for good design. Several of the Herter Brothers' Renaissance Revival pieces illustrated in this book use contrasting wood colors, a fairly unusual touch for the style as a whole (see Fig. 4-11). This use of extra contrast reflects the Néo-Grec style, with which Christian Herter would have been familiar since he had spent time in Paris.

Fig. 4-11 Renaissance Revival figured maple and rosewood library or salon table, c. 1870. Top with rounded corners and felt writing surface above frieze with one long drawer and false drawer on other side. Incurved legs with inverted trumpet and out-flared stylized bracket feet joined by interlaced stretcher with rosettes. Made for a California residence by Herter Brothers. 46″ long × 28″ high. *Courtesy Butterfield & Butterfield, Los Angeles.* **$5,000–7,500.**

Factory Production

The makers mentioned here represent the most collectible segment of Renaissance Revival furniture. Their pieces are sought by collectors and found in the best antiques shops in America. Much more common are the vast quantities of factory-made Renaissance furniture, which can be found in every small shop, antiques mall, and flea market in the country. Factory-produced Renaissance Revival suites found a ready market with the general public even when the reform ideas of Charles Eastlake were being introduced during the 1870s. These factory-made suites for the bedroom, parlor, and dining room continued to be popular well into the 1880s.

A fine Renaissance Revival walnut and ebonized portfolio stand, c. 1865, inlaid with musical trophies. Bronze medallion-mounted crest above fluted canted supports. 40″ high × 23″ wide. *Courtesy Neal Auction Co., New Orleans, Nicolay & Morgan photographers.* **$2,500–3,500**.

Renaissance Revival walnut firescreen, c. 1870, with ferns pressed between glass panes. Crest with "ears," acanthus scrolls, pedimented medallion. Stiles flanked by turned, reeded standards. Resting on an urn-shaped shaft flanked by four turned and reeded uprights ending in four outward-arcing feet. All with incised lines. 50½″ high × 23″ wide. *Private collection.* **$600–900**.

Transitional Rococo-Renaissance mahogany Lincoln rocker, c. 1860. The Lincoln rocker has the same curving form as the Grecian rocker, but with upholstered seat, back and arm pads. It gets its name from the rocker in which President Lincoln was sitting when assassinated. This one with scrolling acanthus arm terminals and rose-carved crest. Note the elaborate scroll flipping up from the roll of the arm—sometimes these are called "whale's tails" when found on formal or country rockers of this vintage. Several Cottage furniture examples with partial "tails" can be seen in Chapter 2. 40″ high × 19″ wide × 20″ deep. *Private collection.* **$475–675.**

Renaissance Revival carved rosewood ottoman, c. 1860, in the manner of J. and J. W. Meeks, New York City. With molded and canted square frame upholstered in tufted wine silk damask, raised on highly carved scalloped and gadrooned baluster-form legs joined by curved stretchers to a central roundel. 23″ wide × 19½″ high. *Courtesy Neal Auction Company, New Orleans, Nicolay & Morgan photographers.* **$750–1,200.**

Left: Faux-ebonized rosewood folding carpet chair, labeled on stretcher "E. W. Vaill/Patentee and Manufacturer/Worcester, Mass./Patented April, 1873." This company was one of the largest chair manufacturing firms of that time. Bears original flower and fern tapestry. 17″ wide × 20″ deep × 31½″ high. **$250–450**. Right: Renaissance Revival walnut canterbury, c. 1875, with gilt, black and green decoration. Shaped top contains four compartments and has one central drawer to a scalloped apron which rests on trumpet feet. 23″ wide × 14½″ deep × 21½″ high. *Courtesy New Orleans Auction Company, New Orleans.* **$600–900**.

Walnut Renaissance Revival side chair, c. 1860, with beaded and molded chair back surmounted by crest featuring dolphins and cabochon set in scrolling plumes. Seat rail with cabochon and scrolls. Turned front legs, on rollers. 40½″ high. *Private collection.* **$350–475**.

One of a pair of walnut Renaissance Revival hall chairs, c. 1860, with pediment topped by shield and scrolling acanthus. Back with burl panel, applied roundels. Legs with applied roundels and palmettes, and ending in hoof feet. 41″ high. Hall chairs and other furniture for the hall (intended not for comfort but for making formal statements) are often highly architectural, showing the true origins of the Renaissance Revival style. *Private collection.* **$900–1,500** the pair.

Walnut transitional Rococo-Renaissance balloon-back chair, c. 1860. With typical finger molding of the Rococo style, and burl panel and crest of the Renaissance style. *Courtesy Eileen Zambarda, 64 East Antiques, Asheboro, N.C.* **$400–600**.

Renaissance Revival walnut hall chair, c. 1860, with architectural back with broken pediment over panelled back with tassel accents. Hinged seat lifts for storage of gloves, etc. (an option on hall chairs). Legs strongly turned. Apron with boss and strapwork-type applied carving. 19″ wide × 17½″ deep × 44″ high. *Courtesy Frederick Craddock III Antiques, Lynchburg, Va.* **$450–650**.

Detail of chair at top right on page 89. Construction note: Chairs from this era were put together with dowels—resulting in a comparatively weak joint.

Walnut Renaissance Revival lady's parlor chair, c. 1870, with burl panels, applied roundels, incised line decoration. Bracket arms. Reeded, trumpet-turned legs (lacking casters). Factory made. *Courtesy Depot Antiques, Hillsborough, N.C.* **$300–450**.

Walnut Renaissance Revival gentleman's parlor chair, c. 1870–80, with ebonized accents, burl panels, incised line decoration, trumpet-turned front legs. Factory made. *Courtesy Carolina Antique Mall, Raleigh, N.C.* **$350–550**.

Walnut Renaissance Revival lady's parlor chair, c. 1870, with tufted upholstered back. Stiles and crest with applied burl panels and stylized acanthus carving. Bracket arms or "elbows" with incised line decoration. Round upholstered seat above trumpet-turned legs. Factory made. *Courtesy Depot Antiques, Hillsborough, N.C.* **$250–350**.

Renaissance Revival lady's chair, c. 1870, possibly by George Hunzinger, New York (the crest with its roundels and emphatic joints is reminiscent of his work). A combination of marquetry, ebony, gold incising, and burl walnut make for a finely ornamented chair. *Courtesy 19th Century America, Lafayette, La.* **$2,500–3,500**.

Renaissance Revival armchair frame, Pottier and Stymus, New York City, c. 1860. Crest rail flanked by two bronze griffin-head mounts, continuing to incised decorated stiles joined by arm rests terminating in bronze cherub heads, resting on shaped seat frame, centered with a Bacchus mask bronze mount on parcel gilt legs, terminating in hoofed feet. 28″ wide × 24″ deep × 42″ high. *Courtesy Neal Auction Company, New Orleans, Nicolay & Morgan photographers.* **$5,000–7,500**.

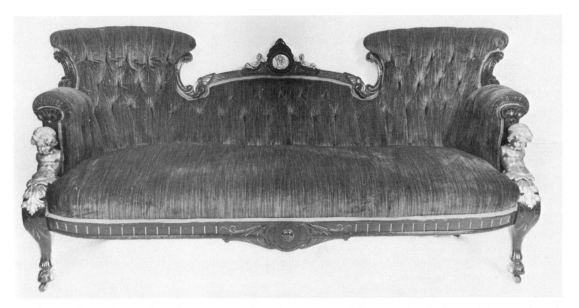

Renaissance Revival tripartite sofa, c. 1865, attributed to Pottier and Stymus, New York City. Rosewood, with gilt-metal mounts, "reeded" apron, cherubs above hoof feet and tufted back. *Courtesy Joan Bogart, Rockville Centre, N.Y.* In restored condition. Dealer estimate: **$3,000–5,000**. (The same sofa sold for $1,000 in 1980 at auction, which gives you an idea of the recent market for quality Victorian furniture.)

A fine c. 1865–75 walnut Renaissance Revival side chair with fine carving (from a parlor suite). Closely related to a set at the Newark Museum. *Courtesy Witherell Americana Auctions, Elk Grove, Calif.* **$1,200–1,800**.

93

Pair of Renaissance Revival lady's chairs (related to a chair at the Houston Museum of Fine Arts and closely related to the sofa in the next photograph). Elaborately carved—note the snarling animal-head arm rests, as well as the Néo-Grec motif of the palmette on the crest and seat rail. Trumpet-turned and carved front legs. On casters. *Courtesy Witherell Americana Auctions, Elk Grove, Calif.* Dealer estimate: **$3,500–5,000**.

Walnut Renaissance Revival sofa, c. 1865, with griffin-carved crest rail flanked by acanthus-carved stiles, triple-section back and seat covered in velvet with mask-head arm supports, leaf-carved apron, cylindrical tapering legs. 78″ long. *Courtesy Freeman/Fine Arts, Philadelphia.* **$2,500–3,500**.

Renaissance Revival rosewood sofa, c. 1870, from a parlor suite with triple-back sofa, two armchairs and two side chairs. Mounted with French porcelain plaques. Incised decorations, trumpet-turned legs, roundels, palmettes, drop pendants on arms, seat rails with dropped decoration. Imposing crest rails. Probably New York City. *Courtesy Morton Goldberg Auction Galleries, New Orleans*. Sofa: **$1,800–2,400**.

Chairs from the parlor suite in previous illustration. Pair of lady's & gentleman's chairs: **$1,800–2,400** the pair. Pair of side chairs: **$900–1,200** the pair.

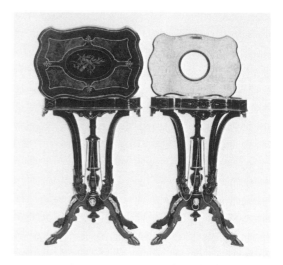

Rare pair of Renaissance Revival work tables. Rosewood, marquetry and burl hinged tops. Open to fitted bird's-eye maple interiors. Base rests on ebonized gold-incised legs with attached ormolu. *Courtesy Witherell Americana Auctions, Elk Grove, Calif.* Dealer estimate: **$4,000–6,000**.

Renaissance Revival smoking stand, c. 1870, of ebonized soft wood, with turned shaft and three attached out-flared legs with applied finials, roundels, and gilt highlights. Lion and ring with chains—a popular motif on small leggy pieces. *Courtesy the Howard Collection.* **$400–600**.

Renaissance Revival walnut oval stand, c. 1865–75, with marquetry top. Top with drop finials, which are echoed in the supports by numerous applied roundels. With lots of incised line decoration. Refinished. *Courtesy Southampton Antiques, Southampton, Mass.* **$1,800–2,400**.

Renaissance Revival ebonized and marquetry side table, c. 1875, probably by Berkey and Gay (one of Grand Rapids's largest firms). Lozenge-shaped marquetry top above conforming apron, raised on ebonized and gilt-incised turned legs joined with stretchers and surmounted by an urn finial. 27½″ wide × 18″ deep × 28½″ high. *Courtesy Neal Auction Company, New Orleans, Nicolay & Morgan photographers.* **$800–1,200**.

Top of Berkey and Gay table, showing the marquetry work.

Renaissance Revival walnut library or parlor table, c. 1860–70, with lozenge-shaped top over base. Frieze drawer. Ball and trumpet turned legs on casters, joined by shaped and molded side stretchers and center turned stretcher. Center of top probably replaced, but not necessarily, since this is a low-end example. 42″ long × 25″ deep × 29″ high. *Courtesy Butte's Antiques, Oxford, N.C.* **$350–475**.

Walnut parlor table with heavy Néo-Grec detail, c. 1875, burl application and inset marble. *Courtesy Witherell Americana Auctions, Elk Grove, Calif.* Dealer estimate: **$1,800–2,500**.

Renaissance Revival figured maple and rosewood sewing table, c. 1870. Top with molded edge over single drawer. Raised on fluted columnar supports joined by shaped stretcher, on stylized bracket feet (casters replaced). Missing sewing basket and one pull. Made for a California home by Herter Brothers, New York City. Herter Brothers, though best known for their Eastlake/Aesthetic pieces, also produced custom-made top-of-the-line work in the Renaissance Revival style. The use of contrasting woods is a hallmark of their interpretations. 34½″ long × 30″ high. *Courtesy Butterfield & Butterfield, Los Angeles.* **$800–1,200**.

Renaissance Revival incised maple sewing table, c. 1870. Rectangular baize-inset top with reeded edge above a frieze drawer and sides applied with figured maple panels and reeded triglyphs above rounded, sliding basket. On reeded trestle supports joined by turned and reeded stretcher. Commissioned for a California residence and executed by Herter Brothers, New York City. 37½" long × 29" high. *Courtesy Butterfield & Butterfield, Los Angeles.* **$5,000–7,500**.

Néo-Grec parlor table, c. 1870, with elongated rectangular marquetry top above a conforming ebonized and gilt-incised apron. Centered with medallion and raised on a pair of tapered columns and pair of griffins all joined to a shaped shelf surmounted by an urn. 43½″ wide × 22½″ deep × 31″ high. *Courtesy Neal Auction Company, New Orleans, Nicolay & Morgan photographers.* **$3,000–5,000**.

Renaissance Revival walnut desk, c. 1870, with eight square-sectioned legs with Renaissance-type motifs, including pseudo-panelling, acanthus and column capitals. Heavy molded stretchers. Frieze with panelling and Renaissance decoration. 58″ long × 31″ deep × 29″ high. *Private collection.* **$1,200–1,800**.

Renaissance Revival parcel-gilt and carved rosewood center table, c. 1870. Shaped rectangular top inset with a leather reserve over gilt-incised leaf-carved frieze fitted with two drawers, carved griffin supports on palmette-carved stretcher. On massive paw feet. Possibly by Herter Brothers. 4'7" long × 30½" high. *Courtesy Butterfield & Butterfield, Los Angeles.* **$7,500–10,000**.

An unusual rosewood ivory-inlaid table, New York, c. 1865. Square top and frieze with extensive marquetry depicting birds and flowers. Supported by central turned and inlaid shaft with four strongly curving legs decorated with scrolls and rosettes. Top lifts up. *Courtesy Joan Bogart, Rockville Centre, N.Y.* Dealer estimate: **$8,000–12,000**.

Simple c. 1865 factory-made Renaissance Revival side table with slightly shaped marble top and conforming frieze. Centered undulating legs flank turned pedestal. *Private collection.* **$250–350**.

Construction note: On this table it is easy to see the most common method of joinery from the era: dowels.

Renaissance Revival walnut parlor table, c. 1860–70, with oval top and molded frieze. Supported by flat, molded legs of undulating form joined by central urn and flaring outward at base. Factory made. 27″ long × 29½″ high. *Courtesy The Antiques Emporium, Raleigh, N.C.* **$300–450**.

Walnut Renaissance Revival center table, c. 1860–70, with oval marble top. Frieze with shallow-carved motifs. Central support with turned shaft surrounded by four molded legs of undulating silhouette and applied carving. On casters. *Courtesy Rudy's Antiques, Virginia Beach, Va.* **$600–900**.

The same idea as in two previous tables taken further, with more decorative understructure. Made by Kingman and Murphy, New York, 1868–72. With three such closely related tables, one wonders whether they were produced by the same factory or by different factories which each purchased turned and shaped pieces from a specialized firm. Since factories all over the country used the same machines, this led to a certain similarity in decorative motifs. But again, the same motifs can be put together to achieve different looks. The interface between mechanization and designers permitted no small measure of variety. *Courtesy Witherell Americana Auctions, Elk Grove, Calif.* **$2,300–4,000**.

A table very similar to previous example, though with a plain frieze and more pleasing proportions. *Courtesy Southampton Antiques, Southampton, Mass.* **$700–1,200**.

Renaissance Revival parlor table, c. 1865, with oval top of inset rouge marble. Frieze with crossbanding and dropped decoration. Unusual base of four centered supports with buttress-like outer elements surrounding turned pedestal and resting on four legs which arc down and end in roundels and molded round coasters. All with crossbanded accents and gilt highlights. 41″ long × 28″ high. *Private collection.* **$1,500–2,500**.

Walnut Renaissance Revival parlor table, c. 1865, with round white marble top. Molded apron with ovals (the effect is of gems set in jewelry) and drop finials. Four centered turned legs mounted on molded double C-scrolls, on casters, and surrounding a pierced urn. 25″ diameter × 30″ high. *Courtesy the Howard Collection.* **$1,000–1,500**.

Renaissance Revival walnut three-drawer bachelor's chest, c. 1860, with ovolo molding, wood foliate handles, wood top. Piece is divided by band of molding below top drawer. Panelled sides. *Courtesy Woodbine Antiques, Oxford, N.C.* **$450–650**.

Renaissance Revival walnut and bird's-eye maple tall chest of drawers, c. 1870, with seven graduated panelled drawers with brass and ebonized drop pulls with molded shaped top and chamfered panelled sides. 45" wide × 21" deep × 70" high. *Courtesy Neal Auction Co., New Orleans, Nicolay & Morgan photographers.* **$2,400–3,600**.

Renaissance Revival walnut side-lock tall chest, c. 1860. Six drawers with molding and wooden foliate handles. Chamfered, molded corners, one with a locking mechanism. Panelled sides. Molded top. 44" wide × 21" deep × 57" high. *Private collection.* **$1,200–1,800**.

Renaissance Revival seven-drawer side-lock tall chest, c. 1860, with burl drawer fronts, ovolo molding, wood foliate and ring handles, chamfered corners, plinth base. Panelled sides. Dovetails are handmade and drawer bottoms hand planed, indicating origin in a small cabinetmaking shop. Philadelphia area. 42" wide × 22" deep × 5' high. *Courtesy Rudy's Antiques, Virginia Beach, Va.* **$1,800–2,400**.

Renaissance Revival walnut sideboard, c. 1860, with burl panelling, decorative molding, roundels, marble top. Two drawers. Side has panelled door that opens to storage area for table leaves. Handmade dovetails, machine planing. 60″ long × 21½″ deep × 33″ high. *Courtesy Rudy's Antiques, Virginia Beach, Va.* **$1,200–1,800**.

Renaissance Revival walnut sideboard, c. 1860, with plinth base, panelled doors and drawers. Architectural-facade-like upper section with applied carved trophy of fish and scroll and cartouche crest. A modest version of the great sideboards seen at international exhibitions in the 1850s and '60s which were heavily carved with food motifs and trophies of the hunt. Marble top, original finish. *Courtesy Southampton Antiques, Southhampton, Mass.* **$2,400–3,600**.

Close-up of carving on crest of sideboard.

Walnut Renaissance Revival massive sideboard, c. 1865, with base of two cabinet doors separated by a panel, all with burl panels and carved fowl and fruit. Three drawers above. Chamfered corners. Rouge marble top with mirrored back and shelf supported by cutout brackets. Domed crest topped by shield, palmette and scrolling foliage. "Gingerbread" and applied food carving on burl panel on back. Approximately 9' high × 65" wide. *Private collection.* **$5,000–7,500**.

Renaissance Revival D-shaped console, c. 1860, with marquetry doors and drawers. Backsplash with burl panels, carving, and gilt accents. 4'3" high × 4'3" long. *Courtesy Butterfield & Butterfield, Los Angeles.* **$2,500–3,500**.

107

Walnut Renaissance Revival cabinet, c. 1870, with burl panels, colonettes and incised line decoration. Panelled door with molded medallion and foliate carving. Two side surfaces flank higher central surface for displaying porcelains or statues. Plinth base. 20″ deep × 45″ wide × 4′8″ high. *Courtesy the Howard Collection.* **$2,500–3,500**.

Renaissance Revival music cabinet, c. 1865, with lower shelf. Rouge marble top. Mixed wood, burl veneer and ebonizing. Applied music-motif carving. *Courtesy 19th Century America, Lafayette, La.* **$1,200–1,800**.

Renaissance Revival gilt-mounted display cabinet cum sculpture stand, c. 1870. Breakfront outline, central section pediment with gilt-metal plaque. Cabinet door with cast gilt-metal plaque with dancing satyr, flanked by gilt-incised scrolls, arabesques and carved palmette spandrels. Side cabinets with glazed doors and later-painted interiors. On outset base on bracket feet. 5'7" high × 6'4½" long. *Courtesy Butterfield & Butterfield, Los Angeles.* **$2,500–3,500**.

Walnut Renaissance Revival hallstand, c. 1860, with knobs for hats, two arms to hold umbrellas, painted iron drip pans, applied burl panels, incised line decoration. Incorporating a "table" with marble top and drawer. Crest with stylized foliage. 88″ high × 44″ wide. *Courtesy Eileen Zambarda, 64 East Antiques, Asheboro, N.C.* **$1,200–1,800**.

A simple c. 1860 Renaissance Revival walnut hallstand with marble-topped table and drawer, drip pans for umbrellas, pegs for coats and hats, mirror. Fanciful shaping typical of hallstands. Original finish. *Courtesy Southampton Antiques, Southampton, Mass.* **$700–950**.

Small étagère, c. 1860, with three graduated shelves supported by turned uprights. Pierce-carved gallery. 44½″ high × 28″ wide. *Private collection.* **$175–225**

Renaissance Revival walnut étagère, c. 1865, with gracefully scrolling fret-carved crest over central mirror flanked by graduated shelves with turned supports and cutout backs. Molded, curving display surfaces. 7′ high. *Courtesy The Antique Mall, Hillsborough, N.C.* **$1,200–1,800.**

Renaissance Revival walnut étagère, c. 1860, with many irregularly shaped cutouts, some with mirror backing. Turned uprights. Drawer in base below marble surface. 51″ long × 17″ deep × 82″ high. *Courtesy Byrum Furniture and Antiques, Hertford, N.C.* **$3,000–4,500**.

Walnut Renaissance Revival étagère, c. 1860, possibly by Mitchell and Ramelsberg, Cinncinnati, Ohio. Pierced, scrolling crest with fruit carving over domed pediment and more scrolls, over long mirror flanked by graduated shelves supported by brackets and backed by irregularly shaped and molded cutouts with mirrors (lower cutouts without mirrors). Serpentine marble surface over conforming drawer. 7½′ high. *Courtesy the Howard Collection.* **$6,000–8,000**.

Renaissance Revival rosewood bookcase, c. 1860, with molded cornice over strapwork- and scroll-decorated frieze above pair of glazed doors. Plinth base. Stiles with acanthus scrolls and molding. 49¼" wide × 15" deep × 73½" high. *Courtesy Skinner, Inc., Boston.* **$2,400–3,600**.

Renaissance Revival walnut bookcase cabinet, c. 1860–70. Base with two panelled molded doors over plinth. Panelled sides. Stepped-back top with two glazed doors. Projecting ogee cornice. Applied acanthus decoration. 9' high × 51" wide × 19½" deep (at base). *Private collection.* **$1,200–1,800**.

Unusual Renaissance Revival walnut writing cabinet in two parts, c. 1865. Upper part with mirrored pediment over central metal-inset and ebony-inlaid fall front enclosing compartmented interior, flanked by semicircular inlaid cabinet doors. Lower part with burl walnut surface and rounded corners fitted with velvet-lined wells, flanking central frieze drawer. On pierced trestle supports. Padded footrest. 4' wide × 5'8½" high. *Courtesy Butterfield & Butterfield, Los Angeles.* **$4,500–6,000**.

Renaissance Revival walnut secretary, c. 1860, with burl panels and oval devices—a favorite shape of the period. Panelled sides. Two glazed doors over fall front over drawer over two cabinet doors. On plinth base. Original finish. *Courtesy Southampton Antiques, Southampton, Mass.* **$3,500–4,500**.

Renaissance Revival walnut secretary-bookcase, c. 1860–70, with molded domed cornice over two glazed doors flanked by scrolling acanthus decoration. Top sides are flush (not panelled). Burl panelled writing surface slides back to reveal fitted interior, flanked by prone griffins. Double-pedestal base on plinth with two panelled cabinet doors and recessed kneehole. Back and base sides all panel-led. *Courtesy Butte's Antiques, Oxford, N.C.* **$4,000–6,000**.

Walnut Renaissance Revival two-door wardrobe in three pieces, c. 1860–70. Domed cornice surmounted by carved bust below anthemion-topped pediment. Doors with burl panels and applied roundels. Chamfered corners. Base with one long drawer with heavy burl accents, molded and cut out to show drawer surface. Panelled sides and back. 52″ long × 20″ deep × 9′ high. *Courtesy Butte's Antiques, Oxford, N.C.* **$2,400–3,600**.

Close-up of the bust-carved crest.

Renaissance Revival parcel-gilt, stained and burl maple armoire, c. 1870, with mirrored door over one drawer in plinth base. Panelled sides. Stiles with inlaid "reeding," also found on frieze alternating with rosettes. Topped by scrolling acanthus. 46″ wide × 7′9″ high. *Courtesy Butterfield & Butterfield, Los Angeles.* **$4,500–6,500**.

Renaissance Revival rosewood wardrobe, c. 1860–70, with arched molded cornice centering heart-shaped urn, with projecting corners. Frieze with rosettes. Glazed door with carved bust of a winged cherub. Chamfered corners with applied carving. One drawer in base over scrolling apron. 51″ wide × 23″ deep × 98″ high. *Courtesy Skinner, Inc., Boston.* **$3,000–4,500**.

Renaissance Revival gilt-incised maple pier mirror by Herter Brothers, c. 1870. Molded cornice over oval medallion gilt-incised with monogram, undulating ribbons and plamettes. Shaped rectangular mirror flanked by two circular platforms with hinged lids, drop finials, and scrolling fluted supports. Base added later. Made for a California residence. 38½" × 7'2" high. *Courtesy Butterfield & Butterfield, Los Angeles.* **$2,500–3,500**.

Walnut Renaissance Revival headboard and footboard, c. 1870. Headpost with shell finial over scroll, foliate and fruit carving, all fitting onto an arched top, with applied scroll and fruit carving, flanked by urn-shaped finials. Footboard with similar decoration. Headboard approximately 55" × 95" high. *Courtesy Frank H. Boos Gallery, Bloomfield Hills, Mich.* **$1,200–1,800**.

117

Pair of c. 1850–60 Renaissance Revival faux-grained rosewood single beds. Headboards with cartouches, flame-urn finials, applied moldings, supported by square-sectioned standards with applied molding. Wraparound footboards rest on turned trumpet feet. 39″ wide × 90″ long × 63″ high. *Courtesy New Orleans Auction, New Orleans.* **$2,400–3,600** the pair.

Walnut Renaissance Revival dresser, c. 1870, with mirror, the applied carvings and decoration similar to bed on page 117. Arched mirror with two shelves, fitting onto a base with three white marble tops, several short drawers and one long drawer. 56½″ wide × 19½″ deep × 86½″ high. *Courtesy Frank H. Boos Gallery, Bloomfield Hills, Mich.* **$1,200–1,800**. Bed and dresser would sell as a set for **$3,500–4,800**.

Dresser with mirror and nightstand from the preceeding bedroom suite. **$6,000–9,000** the set.

A fine c. 1865–75 Renaissance Revival walnut bed with architectural headboard, inlaid reeding, busts of children, burl panels, bronze plaque centered in strapwork-type design. Pediment with palmette and scrolls. Wraparound footboard with beautiful burl panels and bronze plaque. Part of a bedroom suite with following photograph. *Courtesy Morton Goldberg Auction Gallery, New Orleans.*

Renaissance Revival walnut and burl walnut panelled bed, c. 1860, attributed to John Jeliff, Newark, N.J. Central headboard crest bearing carved seated cupid sided by stylized dolphins, caryatids and urns, with three graceful arches enclosing burl panels. Panelled wraparound footboard. 68½" wide × 103" high. *Courtesy New Orleans Auction, New Orleans.* **$6,000–9,000**.

119

Renaissance Revival inlaid maple and rosewood nightstand or bedside commode, c. 1870, with later faux-marble top. Molded walnut border above fluted and lobed columnar supports over bird's-eye maple platform. Base with cupboard door inlaid with grotesques and lotus bands, raised on turned cylindrical legs on casters. Missing drawer, worn. Made for a California residence by Herter Brothers of New York City. 17″ wide × 30¾″ high. *Courtesy Butterfield & Butterfield, Los Angeles.* **$1,000–1,500**.

Renaissance Revival walnut bootjack, c. 1870. We don't see many of these today, but they were an optional feature of the standard bedroom suite, which included several pieces for men: the tall chest of drawers, shaving stand and bootjack. Original finish. *Courtesy Southampton Antiques, Southampton, Mass.* **$800–1,200**.

5

Victorian Ingenuity: Patents and Progress

1850–1900

By the second half of the 19th century, patenting an idea or a design proved to be a dynamic part of American industry and a highly effective marketing tool. A patented item had the air of being the latest thing—the "new improved" version always had an extra edge in the marketplace. Patents for furniture often involved pieces which could be converted from one function to another (a sofa into a bed), or

movable furniture (folding chairs and tables), or simply improvements on an existing design. Except for the output of a few firms like Wooton and Hunzinger, patents generally did not affect the high-style pieces. The appeal of most of this furniture lies in its novelty and ingenuity, not its elegance. Of course, the "novelty" now seems quaint to us, and this has a charm of its own.

Bed

Patents for sofa beds were issued as early as the 1840s, and the innovation was championed in A. J. Downing's 1850 book *The Architecture of Country Houses.* Downing was always in favor of economy, and sofa beds were an ideal way to provide extra sleeping space in a small cottage or apartment. Other designs included folding beds in the 1850s and wardrobe beds, which developed in the 1860s and went through various permutations until the end of the century. Folding beds were among the innovative pieces on display at the Centennial in 1876 (see Fig. 5-1). The

Fig. 5-1 Patent folding bed displayed at the Centennial Exhibition of 1876 in Philadelphia. From James McCabe's *The Illustrated History of the Centennial Exhibition* (Philadelphia: National Publishing Company, 1876).

121

later examples are sometimes called Murphy beds. Probably the least expensive

were the patent lounges, which folded out into beds.

Tables and Chairs

Patents for extension tables also date from the 1840s. This form remained popular until the end of the century and is the dominant configuration for Victorian dining tables. Folding tables date from the 1860s.

The tendency towards specialization in Victorian life led to refinements in manners and furnishings alike and resulted in the development of many new furniture forms created to meet specific needs. For instance, many new types of chairs were introduced. There were window chairs, reception chairs, nursing rockers, porch rockers, platform rockers, folding chairs, reclining chairs, even chairs with perforated backs. There was a corresponding explosion of patents—new techniques led to new forms and vice versa. *The Growth of Industrial Art* (1892), compiled by the U.S. Commission of Patents, stated that 2,596 patents had been granted in the U.S. for chairs and stools alone.[1]

Obviously, chairs were a major area of experimentation, and there were many designs for folding chairs, the first patent for which was issued in 1855. In the 1860s and '70s many other patents for folding chairs followed until this market slowed down in the 1880s and '90s. E. W. Vaill, in business from 1861 to 1891 in Worcester, Massachusetts, had the largest folding chair factory in the world. There were also patents for reclining and swiveling chairs, which offered new levels of comfort for home and office. Patent platform rockers

developed in the 1860s and increased in popularity through the 1880s.[2]

The Vaill factory was located in an area of Massachusetts that had a concentration of chair factories. Gardner and Company (1863–1888) in nearby Glen Gardner, Massachusetts, specialized in producing plywood chair seats. George Gardner received several patents, the most successful of which was for a plywood perforated chair seat. These popular seats were on display at the firm's Centennial booth (see Fig. 5-2) where they were much admired by visitors. Perforated plywood seats proved to be less expensive and

Fig. 5-2 Perforated veneer seats from Gardner and Company at the Centennial Exhibit. From McCabe's *The Illustrated History of the Centennial Exhibition.*

1. Katherine Grier, *Culture and Comfort* (Amherst: University of Massachusetts Press, 1988), 143.

2. David Hanks, *Innovative Furniture in America 1800 to the Present* (New York: Horizon Press, 1981), 33, 36.

122

more durable than caned ones for which they were substituted. The perforations could be arranged in pleasing geometric patterns or they could spell out names, thus providing a new venue for advertising.[3]

George J. Hunzinger

Probably the most widely recognized maker of patent seating furniture is George J. Hunzinger. Although his work can be characterized as Renaissance Revival in style, it is so distinctive that it deserves a category of its own. What strikes one the most about his designs is their innovative quality; his work clearly embodies the Victorian love of novelty. Another one of the influential German immigrants, Hunzinger worked in New York City from the 1860s to the end of the century. (After his death, his children carried on the business until the 1920s.) He patented his designs for folding chairs (he called them "camp chairs"), which sometimes used cantilevered construction. The backs and seats of some of his folding chairs were made of woven steel mesh covered in silk or worsted, an idea he patented in 1876.[4] His chairs—whether folding or stationary—have a strong diagonal element, often with a diagonal side brace (see Fig. 5-3). Many of his chairs have distinctive turnings that call attention to joints. Befitting the spirit of the Victorian age, Hunzinger seems to have drawn inspiration from the machines that fascinated the 19th-century imagination and it is interesting to note how much his turned uprights resemble actual machinery.

Hunzinger's was a very successful business, as is evident from the recovery made after the factory was destroyed by fire in 1877. This comeback was due in part to an 1882 patent for a platform

Fig. 5-3 A George Hunzinger walnut side chair, patented 1869 and stamped on the rear leg. This form is more unusual than some of Hunzinger's designs although it incorporates his typical emphatic joints and diagonal uprights. *Courtesy Joan Bogart, Rockville Centre, N.Y.* **$1,000–1,500.**

rocker with a specific design (Fig. 5-4).[5] Though best known for his patented folding chairs, Hunzinger also made upholstered sofas and chairs that did not fold but still bore traces of his distinctive style. His "lollipop" side chair was patented in 1877.

Wenzel Friedrich

Aside from patent seating furniture, there was also innovation in the types of materials used. Besides wood, there was wicker, cast iron, steel, and even horns from longhorn cattle. One of the best-known makers of unusual chairs was

3. Ibid., 59–61.

4. Art and Antiques, ed. *Nineteenth Century Furniture: Innovation, Revival and Reform* (New York: Billboard Publications, 1982), 126.

5. Ibid., 129.

Wenzel Friedrich, a German who emigrated to San Antonio, Texas, around 1853. Trained as a cabinetmaker, he began to manufacture horn furniture in 1880 (see Fig. 5-5). He won awards at the major exhibitions of the day, and his customers included Queen Victoria and the President of France. His chairs, which were made into the 1890s, were often upholstered in animal hides and furs, including fox and American lynx and Jaguar.

Fig. 5-4 "Lollipop" maple platform rocker by George Hunzinger, c. 1885–95. Bearing the original label: "The Hunzinger Duplex Spring Pat. September . . . 1882/One drop of oil (from your sewing machine can) on every joint or hinge will prevent noise." *Courtesy Neal Auction Company, New Orleans, Nicholay & Morgan photographers.* **$800–1,200.**

Fig. 5-5 Hat rack by Wenzel Friedrich, San Antonio, Texas. In an 1889 catalog he describes a similar hat rack: "The style and general outline of this hat rack will impress you at once with their striking originality and pleasing effect. It contains 32 horns, all framework is horn veneered, has the best French plate mirror beveled edge, also a drawer." A Texas star is inlaid in ivory on the shelf. It sold for an astounding $250. *Courtesy Witherell Americana Auctions, Elk Grove, Calif.* Dealer estimate: **$20,000–30,000.**

Wooton Desks

Office furniture was another important area for innovative designs during the second half of the 19th century. By far, the most prestigious piece of office furniture was the Wooton desk—officially called "Wooton's Patent Cabinet Office Secretary" (see Fig. 5-6). A symbol of the Victorian belief in progress and prosperity, it epitomized the demand for innovation, organization, and gadgetry. This is a wonderfully functional form, and because of its size and bulk, it also served the honorific function that was so valued in Victorian furniture. Its ownership conveyed importance and power; every successful businessman wanted one. They were, in fact, owned by many of the most powerful men of the day, including John D. Rockefeller, President Ulysses S. Grant, Joseph Pulitzer, Charles Scribner, and Jay Gould.

A period advertisement summed up the virtues of the famous desk:

One hundred and ten compartments, all under one lock and key. A place for everything and everything in its place. Order Reigns Supreme, Confusion Avoided. Time Saved. Vexation Spared. With this Desk one absolutely has no excuse for slovenly habits in the disposal of numerous papers, and a person of method may here realise that pleasure and comfort which is only obtained in the verification of the maxim, "A place for everything, and everything in its place." Every portion of the desk is immediately before the eye. Nothing in its line can exceed it in usefulness or beauty, and purchasers everywhere express themselves delighted with its manifold conveniences.[6]

Fig. 5-6 Wooton patent desk, c, 1876–1884, probably an extra grade, with bird's-eye maple interior, decorative gallery with applied panels and carving. Also with walnut and burl walnut. 72″ high × 43″ wide × 35″ deep. *Courtesy Leslie Hindman Auctioneers, Chicago.* **$8,000–12,000**. Depending on grade and condition, Woonton desks can go as high as **$25,000.**

6. From an advertisement in a British newspaper, May 1884. Cited in Betty Lawson Walters, "The King of Desks: Wooton's Patent Secretary," *Smithsonian Studies in History and Technology* 3 (1969): 1.

William S. Wooton sold his popular desks in countries around the world. In 1875 the company employed 150 men, and in 1876 it produced 150 desks per month. During that same year Wooton desks (rotary models and secretaries) were exhibited at the Centennial.[7]

The Wooton patent desk or secretary was produced in Indianapolis, Indiana, from 1875 to 1884. It came in four grades (ordinary, standard, extra, superior) priced from $90 to $750. Each grade came in three sizes, ranging from 4′7½″ to 5′1½″ high and from 3′3½″ to 3′9½″ wide. The form was the same for each, but the standard grade, for example, had veneer panels and better locks than the ordinary grade. The extra grade had incised decoration and a more elaborate pediment than standard, and the superior grade boasted marquetry and a beautifully inlaid interior. When closed, letters could be inserted through the letter slot on some models.

Wooton also manufactured a rotary desk in twelve styles, with single or double pedestal, the pedestals rotating outward to reveal the same kind of vertical slots and cubbyholes found in the Wooton secretary. Some versions had slant tops, others had flat tops or cylinder tops. These varieties were patented around 1876.[8]

Several other manufacturers immediately began copying Wooton's ideas, causing vigorous competition, which may have led to his relatively quick downfall. There were other reasons for the company's demise: by the 1890s typewriters and duplicating machines were in use in business offices, so different office furniture was needed. One central desk would no longer suffice.[9]

Thus the short life of so many patent furniture forms. Epitomizing the Victorian penchant for specialization, many of these oddities have not passed the test of time. What once seemed novel and ingenious now seems quaint at best. But there are many mechanically minded collectors who admire the sheer inventiveness of patent furniture and scour antiques shops seeking out unusual pieces.

7. Ibid., 4, 19.
8. Ibid., 12.
9. Ibid., 22.

Eastlake-style walnut and burl walnut Murphy bed, c. 1880. The bedstead mechanically unfolds from a richly veneered and panelled upright cabinet. *Courtesy Neal Auction Company, New Orleans, Nicholay & Morgan photographers.* **$1,800–2,500**.

Oak patented combination desk/dresser/vanity, c. 1890, with pullout washstand to hold a basin that pulls out from cabinet side. Manufactured by the Eureka Company, Rock Falls, Ill. With Eastlake-type styling, raised panel doors, panelled sides. *Courtesy Pettigrew Auction Gallery, Colorado Springs.* **$800–1,200**.

Murphy bed open.

Oak Murphy bed, c. 1890, incorporating a combination secretary/wardrobe. *Courtesy Pettigrew Auction Gallery, Colorado Springs.* **$1,500–2,250**.

Eastlake-style walnut office armchair on swivel base, c. 1880. Contoured back. Burl panels on apron and crest rail. Spiral-scrolled arms. Bracket-type legs on rollers. Probably "Tyler's Senate Chair" by the Tyler Desk Company of St. Louis. *Private collection.* **$800–1,200**.

Walnut Renaissance Revival child's high chair, c. 1876, which converts to stroller and rocker. Manufactured by Thompson, Perley and Waite, Boston. With perforated plywood seat, back and tray. Perforated plywood benches and chairs were popular in the 1870s and '80s. 32″ high. *Courtesy Whitehall at the Villa, Chapel Hill, N.C.* **$450**.

Late 19th-century bentwood table with shaped and molded rosewood top and decorative, scrolling bentwood base. *Courtesy Joan Bogart, Rockville Centre, N.Y.* **$2,000–4,000**.

Late 19th-century leather-upholstered steer-horn chair. A basic design. *Courtesy Butterfield & Butterfield, Los Angeles.* **$800–1,200**.

129

6

Furniture of Reform: Eastlake and the Aesthetic Movement

1870–1890

The last quarter of the 19th century was marked by reform in furniture design and interior decoration. By the 1870s many had grown tired of the grandness and formality of the Rococo and Renaissance Revivals. What had seemed monumental, heroic and vigorous in the 1850s and '60s came to seem overdone, busy, impractical—even cold. Many decried what they saw as the excesses of revival furniture, especially its emphasis on "showy" ornament, which all too often won out over good principles of design and construction, or what reform writers would refer to as "honest" construction. Above all, "sham" was censured, and "sincerity" was emphasized as a virtue in furniture in popular advertisements and advice books. Ever ready with moral judgments, Victorians invested furniture and interiors with great character-shaping capacities. During the reform era the whole ethos changed, and Americans reinvisioned their homes more as a refuge from the world—a place of sanctuary, comfort and privacy, less a setting for formal public statements. The feeling one wanted to create was more intimate than the grand and formal effect of the revival periods. There was a freer mixing of styles, which added to a feeling of informality. While the Renaissance Revival style continued to be popular for factory output and even dominated the American displays at the Centennial Exhibition in 1876, the real cutting edge was represented by the reform movements.

Why was the country ripe for reform? After the trauma of the Civil War, the country was confronted with a political and economic decline. In the political realm, disillusionment set in with the corruption discovered during Grant's administration from 1868 to 1876. Compounding this was a devasting and severe economic depression that gripped the country beginning in 1873, culminating in the panic of 1893. There were riots in New York City in 1874, a railroad strike in 1877, and many other strikes and riots in the 1880s and '90s. These unsettling events may have contributed to the spirit of reform and the rejection of the highly ornamented, ostentatious styles once so popular.

English Reform, the Aesthetic Movement and Modern Gothic

If America at midcentury had been strongly influenced by French designers, the last quarter of the century brought reform that had its roots several decades before in England. At the time of London's Great Exhibition in 1851, there was general agreement that English design had fallen into a sad state. The historical revivals were bankrupt, and reform was sorely needed. Thus the Aesthetic Movement developed in England during the 1860s. New sources of design provided much-needed alternatives to the overused motifs of the historical revivals. In particular, the 1856 publication of Owen Jones's *The Grammar of Ornament* gave the movement a gold mine of decorative motifs with its catalog of 2,400 different ornamental patterns from all over the world. In another venue, the 1862 International Exhibition in London introduced Japanese goods to the English-speaking world. So different from the dominant western styles, Japanese art proved to be a major inspiration for the Aesthetic Movement. English designers were equally inspired by Gothic designs, and in a surprising twist, found common links between Gothic and Japanese styles. Both were felt to have overall simple, rectilinear form and stylized decoration. Both were felt to embody a kind of purity that was a relief from the hackneyed historical styles.

A romanticized view of English Gothic furniture provided the inspiration for the rectilinear frame and panel furniture of the Aesthetic Movement. Reformers felt that medieval craftsmanship was more honest, sincere and sturdy than that found in the debased revival furniture. And when English designers came in touch with Japanese goods, they saw a connection between the simplicity of Japanese designs and the purity and sincerity they wanted to convey in the decorative arts. The Gothic and the Japanese styles, as different as they may seem to us today, were felt to express the same spirit and embody a union of the useful and the beautiful in the decorative arts. The publication of Bruce Talbert's book *Gothic Forms Applied to Furniture, Metalwork and Decoration* in 1867 (republished in Boston 1873) was an important contribution on the Gothic side of the reform movement (see Fig. 6-1). The Modern

Fig. 6-1 Modern Gothic chest of drawers designed by the Englishman Bruce Talbert and illustrated in his book *Gothic Forms Applied to Furniture* (1867, American edition 1873). His work is very architectural—note the gable with crockets (the little curling pieces) that tops this piece. From *Harper's New Monthly Magazine*, volume 53, 1876, p. 815.

Gothic style owed much to Talbert's work.

Designers like William Morris (1834–1896) and E. W. Godwin (1833–1886) were among those who used obvious construction, functional rectilinear forms and Gothic and Japanese-inspired designs. William Morris placed a premium on handcraftsmanship and the importance of the artisan in crafting fine furniture. This resulted in some stunning furnishings, including fabric and wallpaper, but the products proved too costly for the average person. Godwin's designs, on the other hand, were less predicated on the use of handcraftsmanship and were easily replicated in mass production by English manufacturers. Designs by Morris and Godwin were imported to America during the early 1870s by Daniel Cottier, who had a decorative arts firm in London and a shop in New York City. His firm became an important conduit for the Aesthetic Movement in America.[1]

Charles Eastlake

By far the best-known of the English reformers on American soil was Charles Eastlake. Eastlake subscribed to the branch of the Aesthetic Movement that was devoted to good design without insisting on handcraftsmanship. Eastlake's book *Hints on Household Taste,* although originally published in England in 1868, was far more popular in America, where it was probably the most influential furniture book of its time. The first of several American editions was published in 1872.

The book was not so much a source of specific furniture designs as it was a compendium of advice on how furniture should be made and how homes should be decorated. Eastlake intended the book to teach these principles to a wide audience, not just the elite. As one critic wrote, "Not a marrying couple who read English were to be found without *Hints on Household Taste* in their hands, and all its dicta were accepted as gospel truth."[2] Eastlake's ideas were further popularized by a score of writers who borrowed freely from him. In that way, his ideas became truly pervasive in America in the 1870s.

Eastlake, like other English reformers, believed that construction should be "honest" and designs functional. Honest construction dictated rectilinear rather than curving forms which were constructively weaker. Joints were constructed for strength and not artfully hidden. The emphasis was on sound construction, which determined how the piece would look, rather than the other way around. Fig. 6-2 shows Eastlake's design for a library bookcase that demonstrates several of his ideas.

Eastlake expressed particular disdain for ostentatious "showy" ornament, and furniture that indulged in excessive curving and ornamentation at the expense of sound construction. Perhaps understandably, he reacted against the bountiful curves of the Rococo Revival. He had harsh words for that era:

The tendency of the last age of upholstery was to run into curves. Chairs were inevitably curved in such a manner as to ensure the greatest amount of ugliness with the least possible comfort. The backs of sideboards were curved in the most senseless and extravagant manner;

1. Martha Crabill McClaugherty, "Household Art: Creating the Artistic Home, 1863–1893," *Winterthur Portfolio* 18, no. 1 (Spring 1983): 4.

2. Harriet Spofford, *Art Decoration Applied to Furniture* (New York: Harper & Bros., 1878), 147. Quoted in Mary Jean Smith Madigan, "The Influence of Charles Locke Eastlake on American Furniture Manufacture, 1870–90," *Winterthur Portfolio* 10 (1975): 1.

Fig. 6-2 Library bookcase from Charles Eastlake's *Hints on Household Taste* (Plate XX, 1878 edition). This piece displays the features we associate with Eastlake: rectilinear form, reeded molding, panelling, decorative strap hinges, shallow-carved stylized floral designs.

the legs of cabinets were curved, and became in consequence constructively weak; drawing-room tables were curved in every direction, . . . and were therefore inconvenient to sit at, and always rickety.[3]

As for ornamentation, Eastlake advocated shallow carving and primarily incised line decoration, but never naturalistic carving that was truly representational or lifelike, as was the case with the Rococo Revival era. The exuberant high-relief carving that characterized Rococo Revival furniture and some Renaissance Revival furniture did not have a place in Eastlake's aesthetic. Eastlake believed that "the art of the decorator is to typify, not represent, the works of nature, and it is just this difference between artistic abstraction and pseudo-realism which separates good and noble design from that which is commonplace and bad."[4] Eastlake's decorative motifs tended to be geometric or abstract depictions of nature. Or he might use turned pieces—either as uprights or halved and applied as decoration—to give relief to the overall rectilinear nature of his designs. On fine-quality pieces, he considered marquetry, other forms of inlay and veneering to be suitable.

Eastlake set out to educate the public on points of good design, understanding that mechanization could not be avoided and even made possible the wider availability of better-quality furniture for various budgets. Although he admired the sturdy construction techniques used during the Middle Ages on Gothic furniture, he did not advocate returning to hand work. He knew that mechanization was inevitable in the production of furniture, and he realized that it could make good-quality furniture more affordable for more people. It was not mechanization that Eastlake objected to, but machine-driven designs and the unbridled decoration of furniture that was made possible by factory production. He particularly objected to "wood-mouldings . . . by the yard, leaf-brackets by the dozen, and 'scroll-work' . . . by the pound"—so essential to furniture of the historical revivals.[5]

---

3. Charles Eastlake, *Hints on Household Taste* (New York: Dover, 1969, a reprint on the 4th edition of 1878), 55–56. Quoted in Madigan, 4.

4. Quoted in Mary Jean Smith Madigan, *Eastlake-Influenced Furniture: 1870–1890* (Yonkers, N.Y.: Hudson River Museum, 1973), page 2.

5. Ibid., 58. Quoted in Madigan, 3–4.

Factory Eastlake Furniture

Although Eastlake's book was wildly popular in America, the factory-made furniture that bears his name in this country often departs from his dictates. Somewhat unfairly, the term "Eastlake" is often associated with cheap factory furniture of the 1870s and '80s. We call it Eastlake when it is rectilinear and has shallow, incised, stylized decoration, and perhaps spindles—all things he favored. However, factory Eastlake tends to run riot with quantities of applied ornament that would have offended Eastlake himself. In fact, in the 4th British edition of his book, Eastlake made a point of distancing himself from American factory interpretations— what the Americans "are pleased to call 'Eastlake' furniture, with the production of which I have had nothing whatever to do, and for the taste of which I should be very sorry to be considered responsible."[6]

Of the many factories producing Eastlake-style furniture, very few can be associated with particular pieces. Mitchell and Rammelsberg is one of the documented factories that we know produced quantities of Eastlake-inspired furniture. A sizable company, they employed 600 workers by 1870. Their exhibit at the Centennial included Eastlake-type furniture, and they may have been among the trend setters for Eastlake factory furniture. Mitchell and Rammelsberg did not just produce inexpensive Eastlake furniture, however. They also created custom pieces for wealthy clients in their area. This strategy proved so successful that the firm hired an English interior decorator to set up three showrooms in the aesthetic taste, highlighting products made by the firm.[7]

Cabinetmaking Firms

There were also fine cabinetmaking shops in America which created faithful interpretations of Eastlake's ideas. The other strong reform influences show up primarily in the work of fine shops, not factories. For example, the Modern Gothic style, drawing from Bruce Talbert's book, was limited largely to the luxury trade. Strong Gothic motifs did not gain wide popularity with the American public, but we do see fine Modern Gothic furniture produced by a few cabinetmaking firms like Kimbel and Cabus or Pottier and Stymus from about 1875 to 1885. The other component of the reform movement— Japanese design—was also largely limited to elite cabinetmakers, though some Japanese motifs found their way onto factory furniture.

Herter Brothers

Eastlake-inspired designs found their fullest expression in the work of several top-notch firms. The most desirable pieces were made by Herter Brothers, the New York firm which produced furniture for very prosperous Americans on the East Coast and in California as well, including William H. Vanderbilt, J. Pierpont Morgan, Mark Hopkins, Jay Gould, and even the occupants of the White House during the 1870s and '80s.

Gustave and Christian Herter were German immigrants, steeped in European design traditions, which they successfully adapted to American tastes. The firm had its beginnings in the 1850s, when Gustave Herter formed a partnership with Auguste

---

6. Eastlake, xxiv. Quoted in Madigan, 12.

7. Donald C. Peirce, "Mitchell and Rammelsberg: Cincinnati Furniture Manufacturers, 1847–1881," *Winterthur Portfolio* 13 (1979): 219–229.

Pottier for a few years. When Gustave was joined by his half-brother Christian in 1864, the firm's future was assured of great influence in the decorative arts. A very gifted designer, Christian's training in France and travels to England had put him in touch with the latest ideas in Europe, including an early introduction to Japanese design, which was known in Europe about ten years earlier than in America. Japanese influences filtered through the English Aesthetic Movement and became central to Herter's designs of the 1870s.

In 1874 Christian became sole owner of the firm. By this time English reform designs had come into their own, and England and Japan became the principle design sources. Herter visited England in the early 1870s, and from 1875 to the early 1880s the firm's designs followed developments in England. But Herter took the Aesthetic Movement ideas about simple forms and stylized depictions of nature and created designs that were unmistakably his own. His designs often feature stunning marquetry, best displayed in the famous wardrobe he made for the actress Lillian Russell in the early 1880s. With sleek, straight lines, ebonized wood, bold use of empty space and marquetry of gracefully falling chrysanthemums, the piece embodies the principles of the Aesthetic Movement.[8] A table with similar chrysanthemum marquetry is shown in Fig. 6-3.

Because they made furniture for the elite, their marketing habits were not indicative of more ordinary cabinetmakers. They did not exhibit at the 1876 Centennial, for example, nor did they advertise widely. They were able to attract a wealthy clientele simply by their impeccable reputation as one of the leading tastemakers of the 1870s. The firm's showrooms occupied a prime location in the very fashionable part of Broadway known as the Ladies' Mile, where Tiffany, Lord & Taylor, Sypher & Company, and other prestigious shops were located. In 1874 Christian also built a large factory near Bellvue Hospital.[9]

Publication of the book *Herter Brothers: Furniture and Interiors for a Gilded Age,* by Howe, Frelinghuysen and Voorsanger (Harry N. Abrams, New York, 1994)—and the stunning travelling museum exhibition which accompanied publication—will no doubt increase the already avid interest in furniture made by the Herter Brothers. Their consistently fine style and good construction makes Herter Brothers a standout among Victorian furniture makers.

Pottier and Stymus

Perhaps Herter Brothers' closest competitor was the firm of Pottier and Stymus of New York City. Auguste Pottier and William Pierre Stymus worked together from the 1860s through the '70s as one of the most prominent New York cabinetmaking and decorating companies. Pottier had been in partnership with Gustave Herter in the early 1850s, but went on to form other highly successful partnerships. Pottier and Stymus joined together in 1859. During the 1860s they were known for highly ornamented Néo-Grec cabinets, but they kept pace with fashion and produced Modern Gothic furniture in the 1870s (see Fig. 6-4). In 1871 they built a large impressive factory, which took up almost an entire city block. With showrooms on the first floor, this multistoried building also housed the workshops for cabinetmakers, bronzers, upholsterers, interior woodwork, etc. By 1875 the firm did over $1.1 million in annual sales and employed 700 men and 50 women (who

---

8. Katherine S. Howe, Alice Cooney Frelinghuysen and Catherine Hoover Voorsanger, *Herter Brothers: Furniture and Interiors for a Guilded Age* (New York: Harry N. Abrams, 1994), 49–50, 194–95.
9. Ibid., 70.

Fig. 6-3 A fine c. 1870 ebonized Herter writing table from a signed three-piece Herter bedroom set. An amalgam of the Aesthetic Movement, the Japanese taste and Eastlake—with simple rectilinear form, incised decoration, and inlaid panels of stylized chrysanthemums (an Oriental motif). Stretchers with spindles, and central shelf stretcher. On rollers. *Courtesy Joan Bogart, Rockville Centre, N.Y.* Dealer estimate with matching bed and nightstand: **$25,000–35,000**. Table above: **$4,000–6,000**.

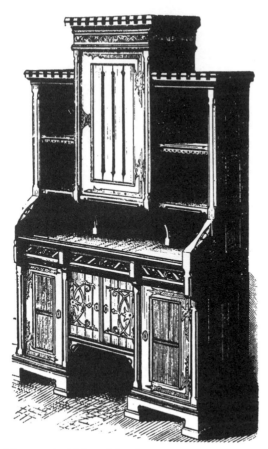

Fig. 6-4 A sideboard by the prestigious New York firm of Pottier and Stymus, another purveyor of the Modern Gothic style. Rectilinear form, with decorative strap hinges, panelling (including linenfold on the side), projecting upper elements, crenelated tops. From *Harper's New Monthly Magazine,* volume 53, 1876, p. 827.

However, clearly much handwork was still needed, particularly on the high-quality goods, and so the carving was largely done by hand. Carvers were among the most skilled and highly paid of those employed in cabinetmaking shops.[11]

Kimbel and Cabus

The founders of the New York firm of Kimbel and Cabus were also part of the wave of European immigrants from the 1840s. Anton Kimbel (1822–1895), a German whose father was also a furniture maker, studied in Germany, Paris and even Russia before he emigrated to New York City in 1848, where he worked with Charles Baudouine's firm from 1848 to 1851. Kimbel was then financed by his uncle until 1865, at which time he went into a partnership with Joseph Cabus that lasted until 1882.[12] Cabus's background was in cabinetmaking, and he had worked with Alexander Roux.

Kimbel and Cabus produced mainly Renaissance Revival and Modern Gothic furniture. They were strongly influenced by Bruce Talbert's book *Gothic Forms Applied to Furniture, Metalwork and Decoration* (1867). The Modern Gothic style included flying buttresses, crockets and finials, columns, projecting or cantilevered elements (like shelves), coves, incised decoration (gilt or plain), and brass strap hinges. The interpretations by Kimbel and Cabus were marked by ebonized cherrywood, which was incised with gilt highlights and decorated with inset tiles. Kimbel and Cabus were one of the few American firms known for this style which was, however, very popular in England during the 1870s.

The Kimbel and Cabus display at the

worked with the fine tapestries and upholstery fabrics imported from France).[10]

Although New York furniture manufacturers were relatively slow to harness steam power to their advantage, during the 1870s it became more common. In 1875 Pottier and Stymus boasted a 150-horsepower engine to run their machines.

---

10. Ibid., 70–74.

11. Ibid., 70–74.

12. Ibid., 26–27.

Centennial included an entire "Modern Gothic" drawing room complete with furniture and wall and ceiling treatments (see Fig. 6-5). This phenomenon of room displays seems to have begun at the Centennial, and it contributed to the notion of interior decoration whereby firms provided not just individual pieces, but an entire look. Kimbel and Cabus also made furniture in the Renaissance Revival style through the 1870s. They generally produced fine furniture in limited stock—in slightly more volume than custom makers like Herter Brothers.

Daniel Pabst

Daniel Pabst, also a German immigrant, arrived in the United States in 1849 and produced his own distinctive brand of Modern Gothic furniture. Around 1854 he set up a cabinetmaker shop in Philadelphia, where he became known as a virtuoso carver. In the 1860s he worked in the Renaissance Revival style and in the 1870s in the Modern Gothic style, obviously influenced by Bruce Talbert's designs. Some of Pabst's work involved executing designs by Philadelphia architect

Fig. 6-5 The Kimbel and Cabus room display at the Centennial Exhibition of 1876, featuring what was called Modern Gothic furniture (it is also in agreement with Eastlake's ideas). Several characteristics which are typical of the style: the mantel with projecting supports, use of decorative spindles, and architectural motifs like the gabled top of the cabinet on the right. From an article by Harriet Prescott Spofford on "Mediaeval Furniture" in *Harper's New Monthly Magazine,* volume 53, 1876, p. 826.

Fig. 6-6 Rosewood library table, c. 1880, with brass and mother-of-pearl inlay. An interesting and unusual mixture of design motifs—with a Louis XVI–shaped top and brass mounts, Renaissance legs and base. The top inlay of a spider in its web, dragonfly and butterflies, was inspired by the Japanese exhibit at the Centennial in 1876. Many details, especially the top, are very similar to work by A. and H. Lejambre of Philadelphia. The mingling of different styles is characteristic of the Aesthetic Movement, although the form is rare. Original finish. *Courtesy Southampton Antiques, Southampton, Mass.* **$4,500–6,000**.

Frank Furness, who may have influenced Pabst to move into the Modern Gothic style (see color section).[13]

Anna and Henry Lejambre

The firm of Anna and Henry Lejambre made a wide range of furniture styles in Philadelphia from 1865 to 1907. Early in their history, the company imported and manufactured French-style furniture and also sold upholstery. Their later pieces reflect the reform styles, including the Japanese taste. The library table illustrated in Fig. 6-6 is closely related to their work.

Japanese Design

Japanese design is another part of the reform movement that impacted smaller firms. Factory-made pieces were largely unaffected by this movement. Japanese-style pieces were only a portion of the output of small cabinet shops and a few factories, never dominating the American market. Americans began to learn about Japan after Commodore Matthew Perry opened relations with that country in 1854. Shortly after that, Japanese goods were exhibited at the 1862 London Exhibition. In America, the craze was fueled by the many Japanese items on display at the Centennial Exhibition in 1876 in Philadelphia, where millions of Americans were introduced to Japanese motifs such as cranes, butterflies, cherry blossoms, fans and chrysanthemums. Following the Centennial, Japanese motifs became popular, and Japanese bazaars could be found around America during the 1880s.

There were several firms that were known for their pieces in the Japanese taste and a few companies dealt in bamboo furniture. For example, the Brooklyn, New York, firm of Nimura and Sato imported Japanese bamboo furniture and locally produced faux-bamboo pieces out of maple.[14] The American Bamboo Company of Boston also manufactured faux-bamboo

13. Doreen Bolger Burke et al, *In Pursuit of Beauty: Americans and the Aesthetic Movement* (New York: Rizzoli International Publications, 1986), 460.

14. Oscar P. Fitzgerald, *Three Centuries of American Furniture* (Englewood Cliffs, N.J.: Prentice-Hall, 1982), 254.

pieces using maple.[15] A. A. Vantine & Company of New York imported Japanese bamboo furniture, as did J. Lavezzo and Bros. of New York. James E. Wall of Boston imported bamboo and lacquer panels to create Japanese-style furniture during the 1880s.[16] Faux-bamboo bedroom suites are the items most commonly found today (see Fig. 6-7). The light, airy qualities of bamboo were considered health-promoting and conducive to a restful atmosphere—ideal for bedrooms.

Fig. 6-7 Maple faux-bamboo bed, c. 1880, Japanese inspired but with Renaissance-style raised panel arches (outlined in "bamboo" moldings). Shallow-carved bamboo and fan motifs on headboard and footboard. 59½" wide × 72½" long. Some veneer damage. *Courtesy Skinner, Inc., Boston.* **$1,200–1,800.**

---

15. William Hosley, *The Japan Idea: Art and Life in Victorian America* (Hartford, Conn.: Wadsworth Atheneum, 1990), 142.

16. Burke et al, 479.

The Household Art Movement

The concept of "home" went through the cultural shift prevalent from midcentury to late century. Home became a retreat from the hectic pace of modern life. Before the Civil War Americans celebrated technological progress with unabashed pride, but by the 1880s, they sought a respite from the fast pace of mechanized life. To defend against the less-positive aspects of modern life, writers (many of them women) sought to emphasize the centrality—we could even say the sanctity—of the home. Home was no longer a place for ostentatious display of one's wealth, but a moral—even spiritual—force directed against a rapidly changing and often disturbing world.

Eastlake and others of the reform movement believed in the power of one's surroundings to act as a moral force that could influence one for the better. Beauty and usefulness and morality were all bound up together. The reformers looked back on the revival furniture of midcentury and saw not just over-ornamentation, but "sham" and dishonesty—harsh words for furniture. Eastlake and others used words like "sincere," "honest," and "truthful" to describe the furniture they admired.

This concern with the character-shaping effects of interior design was part of the Household Art Movement—interior design with lofty aims, reaching beyond mere decoration. The Household Art Movement was America's answer to the Aesthetic Movement in England. In America, concerns had less to do with idealistic goals of handcraftsmanship and more to do with the moral benefits of beauty— the character-shaping qualities of home furnishings. A spokeswoman for the movement wrote:

Its study is as important, in some respects, as the study of politics; for the private home is at the foundation of the public state.... The art of furnishing comprehends much more than the knack of putting pictures and tables and chairs into a suitable co-relation; it comprehends a large part of making the home attractive and shaping the family with the gentle-manners that make life easier to one and pleasing to all.[17]

This type of "art furniture" included the best of Eastlake and Aesthetic Movement pieces—furniture that was dominated by straight lines, with surface ornament, and spindles for decoration.

The interior spaces of houses began to change, reflecting more emphasis on comfort and informality. Configuration of interior spaces moved to a more open floor plan, with less of the rigid separation of spheres that had marked the earlier styles. In this same era the interior decorators first came into their own. Until around 1870, convention associated certain styles with certain rooms, and regardless of the style, it was felt that the furniture should match or be closely related. The reform movement discarded the idea that matching suites provided the basis for a room. A more informal atmosphere was sought— one that was warm and sincere, not cold and formal. An eclectic mixing of styles became the order of the day. Since rooms were no longer limited to one style, a new principle was needed to order a home (it was more complicated). For wealthy clients, the major cabinetmakers began serving as interior designers to bring overall unity to rooms and to the entire home. The large furniture firms—including Herter Brothers, Kimbel and Cabus, Marcotte & Company, Pottier and Stymus, Roux and Company, Cottier and Com-

---

17. Spofford, 232. Quoted in McClaugherty, 6.

pany, and Sypher and Company—added interior design services.[18] For the middle class, advice books were full of hints on the subject.

Household spaces evolved to meet the new informal atmosphere. The hall, once a space for formal presentation and furnished for symbolic impact, became a more inviting space and was often open to the living room. The hallstand was replaced by less imposing furniture. The area once strictly known as the parlor took on new names which conveyed the growing desire for cordial hospitality. "Parlor" changed to "Living room" or the British terms "drawing room" or "morning room" might be used.

In the living room, the symmetrical arrangement of a matched suite around a marble-topped table was replaced with a more eclectic arrangement. Furniture was placed in small groups conducive to intimate conversation. These easy groupings might allow for an Inglenook, a "Moorish alcove" or a "Turkish corner"—tucked away, intimate corners that included cosy comfort.

In this more relaxed mood, the matched parlor suite was scorned—at least by the well to do—partly because it smacked of machine production, which these elitists wanted to deny. Although no longer fashionable with the upper class, people of more modest means still bought parlor suites that were turned out by Midwestern factories in a steady stream up until the end of the century. During the 1870s, the seven-piece parlor suite was a vital part of factory production. By the late 1870s competition between the large factories led to innovation and a demand for new pieces like corner chairs and window seats. By the 1880s the criteria for the par-

lor suite evolved to reflect the fact that it was no longer a requirement in wealthy homes.

The market was strong for inexpensive sets, and a simple way to reduce costs was to reduce the number of pieces. By the 1880s the factory parlor suite was downsized to a five-piece suite. Sometimes a rocker (usually a platform rocker) replaced the lady's armchair.[19] Other changes to suites helped lower costs. The lounge, with a straight back and one raised end, sometimes replaced the sofa—the lounge being less expensive to produce because of simpler designs that required less upholstery.[20] By the 1890s inexpensive factory parlor sets were often produced in a threesome—sofa, armchair and rocker. This inclusion of the rocker was another indication of the move away from the formality that had dominated the parlor for most of the Victorian era.

In this late Victorian atmosphere, the marble-topped center table was no longer welcome, as the overall effect was less formal and any suggestion of coldness was avoided. The use of marble generally fell from favor. The marble mantels and fireplace surrounds were replaced by wood mantels with tiers of shelves for display.

The mantel became a more important focus in the room. Reform mantels were often topped with mirrors flanked by display shelves (see Fig. 6-8). Mantels practically became miniature personal museums. A collection of beautiful objects was thought to add harmony to the home. An attractive Oriental vase placed on the mantel was seen as beneficial to one's character. Bric-a-brac, that wonderful Victorian term for clutter, was not a dust catcher but a way to shape character. Hanging shelves, mantels with shelves

---

18. Burke et al, 116.
19. Grier, 209–10.
20. Grier, 219–20.

Fig. 6-8 Oak Eastlake mantel, c. 1880, with turned and incised decoration. The upper section with shelves and spindled galleries provided display space for art and collectibles—the bric-a-brac so loved by Victorians. Mantels became another focus in the living room (as opposed to the traditional center table) and another place for the display of personal collections, a vital part of the late Victorian living room. 61″ wide × 9′3″ high. *Courtesy Butte's Antiques, Oxford, N.C.* **$1,000–1,500**.

and drawers, wall pockets and wall brackets could all serve to display collections that expressed one's cultivation.

In affluent homes, new rooms evolved during the 1870s and 1880s: the conservatory, which was devoted to culture and natural history; the billiard room and the smoking room—the preserves of men intent on relaxation. The smoking room was something of an American adaptation of Turkish pleasures seen for the first time at the Centennial of 1876. There Turkish bazaars boasted "hookahs" for smoking, comfortable pillows to sit upon, lovely tapestries, and beautiful serving women. Americans were introduced to new ideas about relaxation and luxury.[21] Overstuffed upholstery became popular and was called "Turkish" because it was associated with comfort and relaxation, in contrast to the formality of the tight, buttoned upholstery of the Rococo and Renaissance Revivals. The Turkish fad gained strength with the Columbian Exposition in 1893, where there was an entire Turkish village that featured rooms, a mosque, bazaar and 40 booths selling furniture.[22] In this more cosy setting, the furniture of the last quarter of the 19th century also tended to be less grand and imposing than the Revival styles had been. Yet, as vital as the reform movement was in America, it is important to realize that the broad public continued to have an appetite for richness and ornament, as can be seen in the fad for "Turkish" things. No matter what the opinion of Eastlake or any other reform-minded designer, much of America demanded the lavishly ornamented factory furniture in the Renaissance Revival style (and enhanced Eastlake, as well) into the 1880s. By the 1890s oak fantasies were taking over, with even more carving. The furniture of restraint did exist for a brief time in 19th-century America, but the lure of ornament was never far away!

21. Burke et al., 112.

22. Grier, 193.

Pair of c. 1880 Eastlake-style carved ebonized hanging cabinets, with bevelled glass cabinet doors. One with gilt accents. 12½" wide × 7¼" deep × 31½" high. *Courtesy Neal Auction Company, New Orleans, La., Nicolay & Morgan photographers.* **$500–750** the pair.

Aesthetic Movement ebonized hanging shelf, c. 1880, with stylized geometric incised decoration, including many motifs—houndstooth check, beading, sunburst, pierced stars, strap hinges and pierced Gothic quatrefoil. The Aesthetic Movement in America combined many styles—Gothic, geometric designs and exotic looks such as Moorish or Japanese. This is an appealing factory-made hodgepodge. *Courtesy Morton Goldberg Auctioneers, New Orleans, La.* **$600–900.**

Aesthetic Movement ebonized print rack and stand, c. 1880. Hinged folio panels finely carved with circular panels of floral urns in the Aesthetic taste, with two lower shelves. 22" wide × 35" high. *Courtesy Neal Auction Company, New Orleans, La., Nicolay & Morgan photographers.* **$800–1,200.**

Aesthetic Movement stands and screen, c. 1880. Mahoganized, factory-made. With typical incised lines, stylized floral patterns, "reeding" on uprights. Screen with pierced decoration; perhaps influenced by the Moorish craze. Stand on right with Japanese influence in treatment of the gallery and bamboo-like leaves. Left: **$600–800**. Center: **$500–750**. Right: **$500–750**. *Courtesy Morton Goldberg Auction Gallery, New Orleans.*

Pair of c. 1875 Modern Gothic hall or reception chairs with lift seats to accommodate fans, gloves, etc. Walnut and burl walnut, with ash secondary. *Collection of Dr. Marla Neiman, photo courtesy of 19th Century America, Lafayette, La.* **$3,500–4,500**.

One of a set of 6 walnut Renaissance Revival-Eastlake transitional dining chairs with caned seats, c. 1870s. Chair back with molded stiles, crest rail and splat with applied burl panels. Bracket arms. Turned front legs and double stretchers. While the overall appearance of these chairs is Renaissance Revival, the detailed incised lines and the simplified turnings are Eastlake. *Courtesy Crabtree & Company, Cameron, N.C.* **$900–1,200** the set.

Aesthetic Movement–influenced walnut side chair, c. 1880, with stylized sunflower in back splat and connecting chair rail to high front stretcher. The high stretcher is typical of Aesthetic-influenced chairs, as is the sunflower motif. This is a factory product and much simpler than the custom-made chairs also illustrated in this chapter. The original caned seat is now set with a board and "flat" upholstery. *Courtesy Merrywood Antiques, Richmond, Va.* **$100–175**.

Three of a set of 10 Aesthetic Movement mahogany dining chairs, c. 1880. Repeated spindles were a popular motif with Eastlake and the Aesthetic Movement. Note the high front, side and rear stretchers. Reeded stiles ending in scrolls; similar scrolls complete the arm rests. Interesting turned front legs. On casters. Original finish. Two arm chairs, eight side chairs. *Courtesy New Orleans Auction Company, New Orleans.* **$3,000–5,000** the set.

Two of a set of 12 Modern Gothic walnut dining chairs, c. 1880, (two armchairs and ten side chairs). "Modern Gothic" was the name given to pieces that were rectilinear in form, similar to Eastlake but with obvious Gothic motifs, such as the cutout trefoils, quatrefoils and arches here. This was a later stylistic development than the Gothic Revival of the 1830s and '40s; the Eastlake elements like the shallow, incised carving seen here indicate a date of about 1880. Kimbel and Cabus was one firm known for "Modern Gothic" work—their room display at the Centennial featured the style. *Courtesy Grogan & Company, Boston.* **$3,600–4,800** the set.

An unusual late Aesthetic Movement side chair, c. 1885–90, of chestnut, mahogany and brass. With mother-of-pearl inlay on crest and seat rail. Crest rail curves up and around in the shape of animal heads. Back splat of three vertical pieces. Delicate well-turned front legs. Fine attention to detail, especially in the inlays. With a Moorish feeling that was popular with the Aesthetic Movement. A mate to this chair is at the High Museum in Atlanta, Ga. *Courtesy Joan Bogart, Rockville, Centre, N.Y.* Dealer estimate: **$7,000–12,000** (or you might find one in an ordinary "antiques-junk" shop for $300!)

Pair of ebonized Aesthetic Movement side chairs, c. 1880, related to the following example (a similar crane centers the back splats). Overall rectilinear design, with complex backs broken up by geometric patterns. Reeded stiles topped by stylized sunflowers that create an unusual silhouette for the crest rail—one that is found on other Aesthetic chairs. Overstuffed seats with reeded rails, high stretcher and fretwork. Turned front legs, on casters. *Courtesy Turner Antiques, New York City.* **$1,200–1,800** the pair.

A fine c. 1880 ebonized Aesthetic Movement chair of generous proportions. Back with oval enclosing a crane (a motif borrowed from the Japanese, a major design source for the Aesthetic Movement) and cattails, surrounded by cutout stylized flowering vines. Stiles and rails with repetitive geometric motifs. Front legs turned and with incised decoration, on casters, Brackets connecting legs to seat rail. *Courtesy Turner Antiques, New York City.* **$800–1,200**.

149

Walnut Eastlake-inspired corner chair, c. 1880–90. This rather quaint corner form was introduced late in the period as a novelty item to perk up the standard parlor suite. Arms with stylized floral carving, seat rail with burl panels, dropped apron with incised decoration, turned legs, on rollers. 24½″ × 24½″ × 29½″ high. *Courtesy Eileen Zambarda, 64 East Antiques, Asheboro, N.C.* **$600–900**.

Eastlake sewing or nursing rocker, c. 1870–80, with turned front legs and stretcher, caned seat and back, reeded elbows, stiles and crest, spindles. *Private collection.* **$150–250**.

Walnut Eastlake platform rocker, c. 1870. Stiles, crest and seat rail with incised reeding—basic to most American factory-made Eastlake furniture. *Courtesy Depot Antiques, Hillsborough, N.C.* **$250–350**.

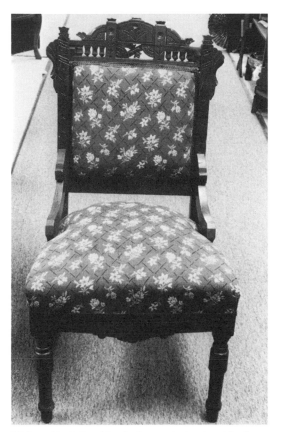

Eastlake-Aesthetic Movement armchair, c. 1870–80, with incised molding and stylized floral decoration. Short "trumpet" legs. *Courtesy the Antiques Emporium, Raleigh, N.C.* **$350–550**.

Walnut Eastlake side chair, c. 1880–90, with decorative crest featuring spindles, fan-shaped pieces, incised stylized flower. With "elbows," turned front legs. 18″ deep × 18″ wide × 36″ high. *Courtesy Carolina Antique Mall, Raleigh, N.C.* **$150–225**.

Drawing room chair featured in Eastlake's *Hints on Household Taste* (1878 edition). With rectilinear form, spindles, incised geometric designs—similar in feeling to the preceeding chair.

Eastlake-Aesthetic armchair, c. 1880. Ebonized wood with gilt incised decoration, "reeding," stylized flowers. Crest rail with spindles. Turned legs. 39" high. *Courtesy Butte's Antiques, Oxford, N.C.* **$475–675**.

Eastlake-type library chair, c. 1870, in leather (as is). Back canted to a comfortable angle and flanked by reeded stiles. Padded arms terminate in roundels and curving burl panels. Trumpet feet, on white porcelain casters. *Courtesy Whitehall at the Villa, Chapel Hill, N.C.* **$1,000–1,500**.

Aesthetic Movement marquetry armchair, c, 1880. Reeded and studded stiles, side rails with repetitive, stylized inlay. Interesting treatment of arms, with "melting" Romanesque columns with lions' faces, acanthus feet, on rollers. Reflecting the Aesthetic taste for the exotic. *Courtesy Pettigrew Auction, Colorado Springs.* **$1,000–1,500**.

Walnut factory-Eastlake settee, c. 1870–80, with shaped upholstered arms, back with incised reeded stiles enclosing two upholstered panels centering a wooden decorative piece. Crest features stylized floral decoration. Turned legs, on rollers. With two side chairs. 53″ long × 39″ high. *Courtesy Crabtree & Company Antiques, Cameron, N.C.* **$800–1,200** the set.

Walnut Eastlake loveseat, c. 1870, with incised arm and crest rail decoration. Applied and raised burl walnut panel on skirt, uprights and crest rail. Refinished and reupholstered. Typical factory interpretation of Eastlake (who would not have curved the arms). 54″ wide × 21½″ deep × 36″ high. *Private collection.* **$400–600**.

Walnut factory loveseat, c. 1890, with two-part back divided by wooden scrolling designs that overflow onto crest rail. Also with some Eastlake motifs: reeding, incised decoration, dropped apron. On rollers. *Courtesy Depot Antiques, Hillsborough, N.C.* **$450–650**.

Modern Gothic walnut octagonal table, c. 1880. Inset tooled leather top with leaf-carved border above a conforming apron pierced with quatrefoils and raised on four canted incised legs joined with a cross stretcher. 36″ wide × 27½″ high. *Courtesy Neal Auction Company, New Orleans, Nicholay & Morgan photographers.* **$400–600**.

Walnut Eastlake parlor table, c. 1880, with marble top. Frieze with incised lines (all machine-executed), drop finials. Base with four central legs joined by X-stretchers, extending to four bracket-type feet. 16″ × 20″ × 28½″ high. *Private collection.* **$275–375**.

154

Eastlake walnut table, c. 1880, with rouge marble top. Frieze with dropped decoration. Four centered legs, each joined to central turned shaft by incised floral panels, and flaring outward. On casters. 31″ long × 22″ deep × 30″ high. *Courtesy Butte's Antiques, Oxford, N.C.* **$500–750.**

Walnut Eastlake table, c. 1870–80. Marble top, reeded frieze with drop finials. Base with four clustered legs centering urn finial and flaring out and downward. Applied stylized foliage and incised decoration on legs. On rollers. 30″ high × 27″ × 20″. *Private collection.* **$500–750.**

Eastlake walnut side table, c. 1880, with white marble top. Legs arranged in X-formation around central shaft and joined by cutout panels. Bracket-type feet on casters, with incised line decoration. 18½″ wide × 27½″ deep × 30″ high. *Courtesy Carolina Antique Mall, Raleigh, N.C.* **$375–475.**

Renaissance Revival-Eastlake oval marble top parlor table, c. 1870. White marble top above shaped incised carved skirt, supported by four galleried legs around a central turned column. 28″ high × 25½″ wide × 19½″ deep. The oval top is very non-Eastlake. *Courtesy Neal Auction Company, New Orleans, Nicolay & Morgan, photographers.* **$400–575**.

Eastlake-style walnut library table, c. 1880, made by Herter Brothers (among those who took Eastlake's principles to their fullest expression in America). Rectangular top with leather inset and reeded edge. Two frieze drawers with reeding. Legs are reeded and turned and joined by stretchers that pass through the legs, emphasizing the joint (a concept favored by Eastlake, who believed that construction should be honest). Spindles (another Eastlake favorite) link stretchers to frieze and add decorative interest. Pull-out slide. Shelf stretcher. On casters. *Courtesy Turner Antiques, New York City.* **$5,000–7,500**.

An important Aesthetic Movement music cabinet by Herter Brothers of New York City. Parcel gilt, painted, inlaid and ebonized cherrywood. Frieze drawers inlaid with stylized flower heads and pierced cast handles over two bevelled glazed lift-up doors enclosing sliding baize-lined sheet music shelves flanked by carved gilt-incised cupboard doors with fielded panels painted with seated muses—Terpsichore and Calliope. Over carved and spindle-set apron on square feet. Back is stamped "HERTER BROS." 8′6″ wide × 34″ deep × 42½″ high. Commissioned for a California residence, c. 1880. *Courtesy Butterfield & Butterfield, Los Angeles.* **$25,000–35,000**.

Walnut Eastlake-type dining table, c. 1880, with reeded frieze. Legs in X-formation around central 8-sided pedestal, joined by fret-carved panels, with vasiform uprights and bracket-type feet. With two more leaves. 48″ × 48″ × 28½″ high. *Courtesy Butte's Antiques, Oxford, N.C.* **$1,200–1,800**.

Eastlake cherry chest of drawers, c. 1870–80. Three over two drawers with incised molding flanked by sides with incised decoration. Panelled sides. On rollers. Original pulls, replaced escutcheons. *Courtesy Antiques Emporium, Raleigh, N.C.* **$400–600**. The same piece in walnut with marble top: **$500–750**.

A well-designed, Eastlake cherry dressing table, c. 1875–80. Rectangular mirror frame set between a pair of drawers resting on lower case having central drawer above an open section fitted with half-shelf and between pedestal ends, each with narrow drawer above cupboard door mounted with strapwork hinges. 49″ wide × 21″ deep × 60″ high. *Courtesy Neal Auction Company, New Orleans, Nicolay & Morgan photographers.* **$800–1,200**.

Walnut factory-Eastlake dresser, c. 1870–80, with two glove drawers flanking inset marble top. Three drawers with incised molding and burl panels. Panelled sides. Mirror flanked by candle brackets, with incised molding, and topped by repeated stylized flower motif and crenelations. "Button and scallop" dovetails, made by the Knapp dovetailing machine which was invented in 1868. 30″ wide × 6′ high. *Courtesy Depot Antiques, Hillsborough, N.C.* **$600–900**. With marble tops: **$750–1,200**.

Eastlake/Renaissance Revival walnut washstand, c. 1870, with one long drawer over two drawers beside a cabinet—all with reeding and burl panels. Case with reeding and incised decoration. Marble top, backsplash with two candlestands, Renaissance-type shaping and crest. 33″ wide × 20″ deep × 48″ high. This is a marriage—the original backsplash was marble. We often naively believe that Victorian pieces are so "new" that they have not suffered the indignities that befall many 18th-century pieces. Not so! Marriages, divorces, splitting of sets, stylistic additions and alterations are all found in abundance. *Private collection.* **$450–650**.

Maple washstand in the Japanese taste, c. 1880, with marble top. Backsplash with Japanese crest over painted panel. A combination of Eastlake-type reeding and Japanese lines—for instance, on the sides, the cabinet doors centering carved panels of birds, and the fretwork below the cabinets. Central cutout shelf stretcher. Made by Mitchell and Rammelsberg, Cincinnati, Ohio, a major factory and producer of well-designed Eastlake, Modern Gothic, and Japanese-inspired pieces. 38″ wide × 19″ deep × 39″ high. *Courtesy Turner Antiques, New York City.* **$2,500–3,500**.

Eastlake walnut side-lock tall chest, c. 1870. Drawers accented with applied burl panels. Plinth base. Top with one drawer and gallery with raised central section, decorated with applied "crenelations." Drawers with Knapp dovetails. 49″ wide × 20″ deep × 63″ high. *Courtesy Butte's Antiques, Oxford, N.C.* **$1,500 2,500**.

Eastlake walnut sideboard, c. 1870–80, with many different types of decoration: marquetry panels of game birds, reeding, molding, rows of repeated incised and cutout geometric designs, spindles and burl panels. Typical of Eastlake is the rectilinear form and stepped-back upper section. Eastlake would not have approved of the birds, however. He would have rendered them in a more stylized, less lifelike manner. Original finish. *Courtesy Southampton Antiques, Southampton, Mass.* **$1,800–2,400**.

Sideboard, c. 1880, from a design by Charles Locke Eastlake, featured in *Hints on Household Taste*. Walnut and tulipwood, original finish. Base on saw-tooth-carved feet with panelled sides, panelled doors with prominent decorative hardware. Central open area framed by an arch, with drawers above. Three shelves above with "bamboo"-turned supports. With painted Minton-Hollis tiles. 76½" high × 54" wide × 27" deep. The number of pieces that are Eastlake style or influenced by Eastlake is vastly greater than the number of pieces copied directly from his own designs. This is a handsome piece and a relative rarity; it will be quickly snatched up by a collector. *Courtesy Turner Antiques, New York City.* **$10,000–15,000**.

Charles Eastlake's design for a dining room sideboard. Plate XI, from the 1878 edition of *Hints on Household Taste*—compare to the previous example.

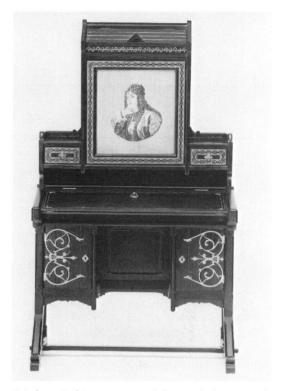

"Modern Gothic" secretary of ebonized cherrywood, c. 1875, attributed to Kimbel and Cabus, New York City. Gabled cornice with gilt-incised decoration opening to reveal a storage compartment above a marquetry-border bookcase door containing a petit point and Berlin-work needlepoint portrait of a maiden and flanked by a pair of galleried marquetry drawers, resting on a lower case fitted with a fold-out adjustable writing surface above a pair of recessed doors decorated with elaborate pierced brass hinges, and panelled sides outlined with gilt-incised fish scales. The whole raised on a canted chamfered trestle-form base. 36½″ wide × 22″ deep × 65″ high. *Courtesy Neal Auction Company, New Orleans, Nicolay & Morgan photographers.* **$2,500–3,500**.

Ebonized cabinet attributed to Kimbel and Cabus, New York City, c. 1880. Strongly influenced by designs from the Aesthetic Movement and especially Bruce Talbert. This piece is also in agreement with Eastlake's ideas, in its rectilinear form, trestle base borrowed from medieval furniture, incised line decoration, inset ceramic tiles, and spindle-decorated gallery. *Courtesy Joan Bogart, Rockville Centre, N.Y.* Dealer estimate: **$6,000–10,000**.

A fine c. 1870–80 Eastlake walnut fall-front secretary or secrétaire à abattant. Panelled fall front and drawer fronts with egg-and-dart borders. Plinth base. Fall front engineered in balanced cantilever fashion. Interior with secret drawer (spring loaded). Well-turned colonettes topped by stylized leaf carving, fish scale carving below. Panelled sides and back. Cherry drawer sides and bottoms. Brass pulls with owl and duck motif. 36″ wide × 20″ deep × 5′2″ high. *Courtesy Rudy's Antiques, Virginia Beach, Va.* **$3,500–4,500**.

162

Eastlake walnut cylinder (rolltop) desk, c. 1870–90—
a popular Victorian desk form. Spindled gallery (typical of the Eastlake style) and reeding are the only
decorations on this simple masculine form. Original
finish and rough condition. *Courtesy Southampton
Antiques, Southampton, Mass.* As is: **$600–900**. Re-
stored: **$1,000–1,500**.

Walnut Eastlake cylinder secretary/bookcase, c.
1870–80, with burl panels, reeding, stylized floral
motif, panelled sides. Poplar interior, with a yellow
wash (typical of Victorian interiors). Original condition. 39″ wide × 22″ deep × 7′2″ high. *Courtesy
Rudy's Antiques, Virginia Beach, Va.* **$3,500–4,800**.

Eastlake walnut cylinder secretary, c. 1870–90, with burl panels. The cornice reflects the American tendency to embellish Eastlake's simple forms. Refinished. *Courtesy Southampton Antiques, Southampton, Mass.* **$2,400–3,600**.

Eastlake walnut bookcase, c. 1870–80, with one drawer below stepped-back bookcase. Incised molding, crenelations. Original ring pulls. May originally have had a gallery. Although this certainly is Eastlake style in terms of overall rectilinear design and decorative motifs, Eastlake actually had specific ideas about bookcases. He felt that they should not have glass doors; instead, books could be protected from dust by curtains or by a narrow decorative leather flap. 30″ wide × 16″ deep × 5′ high. *Courtesy Depot Antiques, Hillsborough, N.C.* **$600–900**.

Eastlake cylinder desk with attached bookcases, c. 1880–90. Walnut, with incised line decoration, burl panels, crenelations, reeding. Desk with bevelled mirror, cylinder top, drawer and cabinet door. Bookcases each with drawer in base and stepped-back glazed door, egg-and-dart-type cornice. Panelled sides. 67″ wide × 25″ deep × 5′10″ high. *Courtesy Butte's Antiques, Oxford, N.C.* **$3,500–4,800**.

Eastlake bookcase/cabinet of faux-grained soft wood, c. 1880. With a crenelated cornice. Two glazed doors over three graduated drawers. Applied roundels. Plinth base. *Courtesy Whitehall at the Villa, Chapel Hill, N.C.* **$1,800–2,500**.

Eastlake-style walnut writing desk, c. 1880. Floral-carved geometric pediment above a rectangular bevelled glass mirror flanked on either side by two small cabinets, recessed behind a lift-top writing surface with inset leather opening to reveal a leather interior with fitted compartment of drawers and cubbyholes, raised on a trestle-type base with recessed shelf. 30½″ wide × 21¼″ deep × 53″ high. *Courtesy Frank H. Boos Gallery, Bloomfield Hills, Mich.* **$800–1,200.**

Cherry or mahoganized maple chiffonier, c. 1880–1900, with attached bevelled mirror with simple acanthus decorations, roundels and Eastlake-type reeded molding. Original finish. On casters. This was a new form during this period, being a variation on the tall chest. Late in the Victorian age a taste developed for whimsical design, with new asymmetrical arrangements of cabinets and drawers. This configuration was taken to its most extreme in the many side-by-sides from that period. *Courtesy Southampton Antiques, Southhampton, Mass.* **$500–750.**

Aesthetic-influenced factory-made mahogany side cabinet, c. 1890. Elliptical top with one long rectangular shelf with a pierced fan-carved ball and spindle-carved backsplash above an elliptical bevelled glass mirror behind two small shelves with ball-and-spool supports. Rectangular top above a frieze of one long drawer above two long doors with carved leaf-and-ribbon decoration, raised on exaggerated cabriole legs. 15″ deep × 17½″ wide × 55½″ high. *Courtesy Frank H. Boos Auction Gallery, Bloomfield, Hills, Mich.* **$500–750**.

Walnut Fort Wayne Organ Company Packard Organ with windpipes, c. 1880. Eastlake incised decoration, Renaissance fretwork. 49″ long × 23″ deep × 70½″ high. *Courtesy Frank H. Boos Gallery, Bloomfield Hills, Mich.* In good working order, **$800–1,200**.

Factory-made pine bedstead and dresser with inset tiles, c. 1880, bringing together several styles, which is typical of late 19th-century factory production. Herringbone effect, tiles, incised stylized floral decoration, turned uprights, drop finials, urn finials, stiffly carved crest. Probably English, but similar to some American examples. *Courtesy Morton Goldberg Auctions, New Orleans.* **$1,800–2,400** the set.

Bed from Egyptian Revival ebonized cherrywood and gilt-incised two-piece bedroom suite, c. 1876. Architectural headboard inset with polychromed and gilt plaque depicting Egyptians, and with panelled section and baluster-turned stiles. Low footboard incised with papyrus blossoms and pseudo-hieroglyphics. Made in New York. Original condition. The Egyptian Revival shows up occasionally from the Renaissance Revival period to the end of the century, grafting onto the current styles— in this case an Eastlake or Aesthetic look. 62″ wide × 89″ deep × 82″ high. *Courtesy Neal Auction Company, New Orleans, Nicholay & Morgan photographers.* (Priced as set with following photograph.)

Dresser matching bed at bottom of page, opposite. Tall cheval mirror topped by polychromed and gilt plaque depicting Egyptians watering a garden. Resting on double marble-topped cabinet bases fitted with four drawers each. Original condition. 83″ wide × 23″ deep × 90″ high. *Courtesy Neal Auction Company, New Orleans, Nicholay & Morgan photographers.* **$10,000–15,000** the set.

Eastlake walnut and burl walnut double bed, c. 1880, with some Néo-Grec touches (such as the anthemion crest rail, columns flanking central burl panel, and drops above columns). The horizontal panels of this bed are typical of Eastlake beds. 74″ long × 52″ wide × 95″ high. *Courtesy New Orleans Auction Gallery, New Orleans.* **$1,000–1,500**.

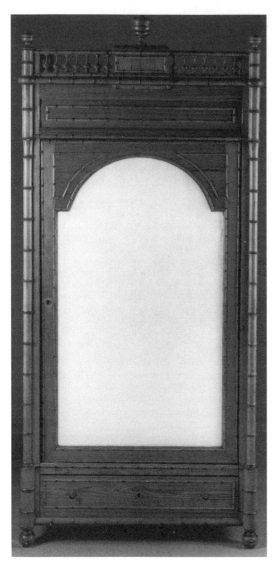

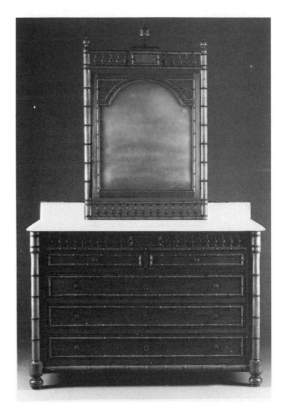

Faux-bamboo Japanese-style chest of drawers, c. 1880. Two over three graduated drawers with decorative frieze which matches gallery tops of other pieces from the set (mirror shown, hanging above chest). Marble top with splash, doubling piece as a washstand. *Courtesy Butterfield & Butterfield, Los Angeles.* Chest: **$1,200–1,800**. Mirror: **$450–650**. Note on suites or sets: Complete bedroom sets *should* bring more than the separate pieces, but often don't! Therefore dealers and auction houses frequently separate them to maximize profit. Sets consist of as many as seven pieces.

Faux-bamboo wardrobe, c. 1880, with single mirrored door and single drawer. Galleried top. (Note following photo of mirror and chest from same set). *Courtesy Butterfield & Butterfield, Los Angeles.* Wardrobe: **$2,400–3,600**. Double wardrobe: **$3,500–4,800**.

Factory-made dresser and wardrobe from a c. 1890 bedroom suite. To call this Eastlake is a stretch—the base of the dresser is factory Eastlake, but the crests have the exuberant carving of the 1890s opulent period. Characteristic of 1890s factory furniture is the real mishmash of styles—Eastlake; spiral turnings from the Renaissance; the crest treatment, headboard and footboard inspired by the rococo. *Courtesy Flomaton Antique Auction, Flomaton, Ala.* Dresser: **$600–1,000**. Wardrobe: **$600–1,000**.

7

Mail-Order Opulence: 1890–1900

In many ways golden oak furniture was a natural outgrowth of the popular factory-Eastlake furniture of the 1880s. Eastlake furniture, with its straight lines and incremental add-on decoration, was easily adapted to factory production. Of course, even in the 1880s factory designers were more generous with ornament than Mr. Eastlake himself would have found tasteful. But by the end of the 1880s, factory styles became even more ornate. Only remnants of the Eastlake idea survived when this extremely eclectic style of decoration and carving began to dominate factory production. This mass-produced furniture was made primarily for middle-class customers, and it needed to be attractive and inexpensive at the same time. The new Midwestern factories with their mechanized production made this dream possible for a large number of Americans.

Many of the factories making golden oak furniture were founded in the Midwest in the 1870s and 1880s. From the start they were equipped with steam to power new woodworking machines. Grand Rapids, Michigan, was probably the most concentrated area for golden oak, although there were also manufacturing centers in Ohio, Illinois, Indiana, New York and Virginia. These factories made huge quantities of furniture, and many of them contracted with the emerging mail-order firms to provide cheap furniture for millions of Americans.

From the 1880s on, this furniture was available through department store catalogs, and especially from Montgomery Ward and Company and Sears, Roebuck and Company from 1893 on. As railroads penetrated more and more of the country, and post offices opened up following the tracks, mail order became a popular way to sell to rural America. As late as 1880, about 70% of America's population was still rural. This was a huge customer base eager for affordable furniture, and mail order proved to be the best way to reach them. Much to the distress of the general stores, Chicago-based companies like Sears, Roebuck and Montgomery Ward began making steady inroads into the rural market. Chicago had its own burgeoning furniture industry with a full range of large factories and high-quality custom shops. Its central location was a key advantage to the great mail-order houses as they set out to create millions of loyal customers all over the country. Extravagant sales copy aside, those companies provided inexpensive furniture. Sears, Roebuck originally purchased furniture from the large factories nearby, but soon after the turn of the century, they actually owned a range of factories, including an upholstered-furniture plant in Chicago.

Another popular variation on catalog sales was golden oak furniture offered as premiums by the Larkin Soap Company of Buffalo, New York—which sold household goods, food, toiletries, notions, and soap. Premiums were used as incentives to purchase Larkin products. The company issued a premium catalog twice a year. One of their most popular premiums was the Larkin desk with slant front and open shelves.

Rural Free Delivery, which began in 1896, and Parcel Post, after 1912, helped make mail-order furniture an option.[1]

From Golden Oak to Fake Oak

By the 1880s the supply of walnut, the favored wood for Renaissance Revival furniture, had been seriously depleted. Manufacturers turned to oak, which was readily available in the Midwest, particularly in southern Illinois and Indiana. Great stands of red oak and white oak were harvested and shipped to factories to be made into golden oak furniture. Oak was strong and durable, but not as easily carved as walnut and mahogany. Mail-order firms wanted strong, sturdy furniture, for which oak was a perfect choice. Often the components were made and shipped to the retailer for final assembly, or parts were crated and shipped directly to the customer.

During this period, oak was treated (finished) in several different ways and was used in solid and veneer forms. Quartersawn oak was very desirable because it produced boards with an attractive patterning of rays. Because the boards were cut to show the most pattern, some timber was wasted, resulting in a more expensive product. Besides its attractive look, quartersawn wood tends to shrink less than other cuts, making a more durable piece of furniture.

One of the drawbacks to oak was its lack of color. The whole Victorian era favored dark woods—rosewood, mahogany, black walnut—so darkened oak must have seemed an obvious improvement to designers in the 1880s and '90s. Various experiments were conducted to come up with attractive finishes. Noticing the effects of tobacco juice on the factory floors, one designer in Grand Rapids tried nicotine stains on oak. This darkly stained oak was called "mud oak" by its detractors, but it proved a strong seller nonetheless.[2]

Fumed oak was the result of exposing unfinished oak to ammonia fumes. Since the fumes penetrate deep into the wood, it is difficult to undo this type of treatment—in fact, it can be a losing battle. Weathered oak, another finish, has a silvery gray look which was produced by using fumes or by simple exposure to the elements. "Antique" oak has a nut-brown finish or contrasting highlights and darker areas achieved by spraying. Golden oak, the most desired finish today, was attained by a hard, orange shellac finish.

While oak was the most desirable wood, furniture made from stained maple or other stained woods—fake oak—was often sold at the low end of the market. Ash, chestnut, elm and hickory all look similar to oak and were frequent substitutes. Inexpensive hotel furniture was of-

---

1. Mail-order golden oak furniture continued to be popular well past 1900, the end date for our book. Golden oak was one of the remnants of the Victorian age that carried over into the 20th century, but after 1900 the Colonial Revival and other styles replaced the Victorian mentality, at least on the cutting edge of fashion. Thus we have chosen to end our coverage of golden oak at 1900, a date which most agree signals a new design era. Our book *Colonial Revival Furniture* (Wallace-Homestead, 1993) covers the new design era.

2. Frank Edward Ransom, *The City Built on Wood* (Ann Arbor, Michigan: Edwards Brothers, 1955), 27.

ten made of various woods and stained to look like the favored oak. Sears, Roebuck and other mail-order kings also sold great quantities of fake oak advertised as having an antique oak finish. Even if you are not an expert in wood types, it is fairly easy to unmask fake oak. When you look at the underside of a table or the inside of a door, for example, the patterns on the outside or top should also be found underneath. If not, you have fake oak.

Settings and Furniture Forms

Through mail order, a family could furnish the parlor in one purchase. By this time the seven-piece suite had evolved into a more affordable three-piece suite, usually consisting of a settee, armchair and rocker. Indeed, the rocker came into its own during this era, with platform rockers leading the way. Once relegated to private areas of the house, the informality of rockers was gradually allowed into the parlor as the century wore on and manners compromised with comfort. Of course, parlors in the countryside always had a character that was different from the formal rooms in sophisticated city settings. Rural parlors might fall prey to a kind of formality that made them unusable except for the milestones of life—like weddings and funerals—or they might be more like living rooms that were comfortable and full of personal touches.

Matching suites were a big seller, not only for the parlor but also for the dining room and bedroom. The basic chamber (bedroom) suite consisted of a bedstead, dresser, and washstand (usually with towel rack). Dining rooms almost always centered around an extension table—either of pedestal form or with legs at the corners. China closets were made by the millions (see Fig. 7-1), and press-backed chairs and sideboards were other dining room furnishings. Ice boxes—usually found in the kitchen—were also common in this era. They were often made of elm or elm veneered in oak.

Practical, sturdy office furniture in oak and other woods, often was made by companies specializing in office furniture. Side-by-sides and Larkin desks may be

Fig. 7-1 Golden oak tripartite china closet, c. 1900, with four paw feet, applied acanthus carving, and scrolling crest. Central convex glass door flanked by two columns with capitals. Upper section with bevelled glass in circle and teardrop design. Oak and oak veneer. The golden oak china closet is another one of those forms that is found in many, many variations. Just about everyone's grandmother seems to have had one! This one is a nice example. 6' high. *Courtesy Butte's Antiques, Oxford, N.C.* **$2,000–4,000**.

quaint and appealing, but the panelled flat-top desks and the rolltop desks are truly practical. Perhaps because of their relative simplicity, attractive style, and usefulness, they are sought by today's consumers as well.

Mass-produced mail-order furniture (oak or otherwise) was one area of furniture manufacturing that took advantage of new steam-driven technologies. The ubiquitous pressed-back chairs (see Fig. 7-2) were, of course, not hand-carved but rather decorated with an embossing machine that was introduced in the late 1880s. The depth of cut was limited to about one inch, and the embossing machine was not capable of undercutting or fine detail. Embossed designs were sometimes cut away from the wood stock and then applied to furniture—a method commonly used on mail-order furniture as an alternative to more expensive carved ornaments.[3]

We might criticize factory production for the weak design, but the freedom apparent in shapes and motifs is really what gives many pieces their charm. One can easily say that these pieces do not make organic wholes. Often the designer simply used whatever carved pieces were available and had workers apply them to any number of forms, rather than planning the decoration around the form and function of a particular piece. This said, however, there is often an exuberance in the decoration that customers clearly loved and that appeals to collectors today. Again, this furniture reminds us that the Victorians loved novelty, variety, and visual surprises—which could take the form of asymmetrical arrangements, irregular shapes, and a great variety of applied carving. Side-by-sides, a good example of this

Fig. 7-2 Simple pressed back oak side chair, c. 1900. 17¾" wide × 39¼" high. *Courtesy Carolina Antique Mall, Raleigh, N.C.* **$40–60**.

aesthetic, are often a tour de force of applied carving, turned pieces and bevelled or stained glass set in eccentric shapes (see Fig. 7-3).

---

3. Michael J. Ettema, "Technological Innovation and Design Economics in Furniture Manufacture, "*Winter" Portfolio* 16 (1981): 221–23.

Grand Rapids

Grand Rapids was a center of mass-produced furniture during this time. However, its output was not limited to the low-end market. Most successful firms had a high-end line which they produced in smaller quantities, using better-quality materials and more hand work. During the 1880s Grand Rapids factories began using mahogany again, generally for their more expensive suites. Demand was strong enough for the Honduras Lumber Company to establish an office there in 1886. A Nelson and Matter mahogany bedroom suite furnished the White House during the administration of President Arthur[4]— surely a testament to the quality of some of the work. During the 1880s original designs were emphasized—as we can see from the whimsical, fanciful pieces illustrated on pages 179–191. Along with the mass-produced items designed to be crated and shipped and made under contract for mail-order companies or other buyers, most factories also produced a line of better goods with which to secure their reputation. These higher-quality pieces might use mahogany or oak and exhibit profuse carving. A newspaper article from Detroit in 1877 commented on the carving:

Each establishment has its own staff of designers and they are busy the whole year round planning articles for furniture as comfortable, unique, and beautiful as the art of man can compass. The designing and execution are alike perfect. The wood carving departments are a wonder in their way. Some of the wood carvers came from Glasgow, having learned their business on the Clyde, carving figureheads, stem and stern adornments and cabin decorations for the mercantile, naval, racing, and pleasure craft of the world. This apprenticeship stood them in good stead. There is no style of carving too intricate for their deft chis-

els. . . . It is an interesting sight to behold a force of thirty to forty of these handcraftsmen employed in one large room, and to inspect the wonderful variety of work executed there.[5]

Along with the skilled carvers on staff in Grand Rapids factories, there were also firms specializing in turned and carved wood ornaments. Power-driven spindle

Fig. 7-3 Mahoganized hardwood side-by-side, c. 1890, exhibiting the pastiche of decorative elements on factory-made pieces of that era: grotesque masks and swirling acanthus, rope-turned corners, irregularly shaped bevelled mirror, bowfront drawers under the slant front, curving glass on the china cabinet door, scalloped apron. A tour de force of whimsical design. 6′ high. *Courtesy The Antique Mall, Hillsborough, N.C.* **$1,500–2,400.**

---

4. Ransom, 24.

5. Ibid., 27.

carvers, capable only of crude carving, were introduced in the late 1880s. Hand carvers were still needed to bring out the details and to do more intricate work on better-quality pieces. Some companies sought out carvers in Europe, as did the Berkey and Gay firm, which procured skilled carvers from Italy.[6]

Custom Furniture

Not all of the furniture from this period was factory-produced. There were also custom shops that made huge, extravagantly carved furniture, sometimes out of oak, but also using the scarcer mahogany and walnut. (Mahogany had begun to make a comeback in the 1880s after almost 30 years of limited use.) Massive is the best word to describe these pieces. Impressive size is one of the hallmarks of Victorian furniture as a whole and it remained true in this last phase as well. Size carried symbolic weight and, clearly, bigger was better. These pieces were meant to convey the owner's economic and social status. Like so much Victorian furniture, the opulent furniture of the 1890s is assertive. The size and extensive carving can be almost overwhelming.

One of the best known of the custom shops was the firm of R. J. Horner of New York City. He worked around the turn of the century in a variety of styles, but is best known for his opulently carved oak pieces (see Figs. 7-4 through 7-7). His work is truly massive and positively encrusted with high-relief imaginative carving of putti, mythical beasts like griffins, dolphins and satyrs. The subject matter is different, but the level of detail approaches the great naturalistic carving of the Rococo Revival period. The figures are not stylized—they are as realistic as such

fantastic figures could be. When the carving is executed in oak, it is somewhat coarser than carving in other woods, simply due to the properties of oak. The overall feeling is robust with Renaissance-inspired motifs such as bust carving, scrolling foliate carving, gadrooning and putti holding scrolls and swags.

The wealthy at midcentury had brought the bounty of nature and its carnage into their dining rooms on massive sideboards. It was an idealized view of nature clearly mastered by man. By the end of the century, the wealthy again were filling their dining rooms with assertive carved figures, but now taken from mythology rather than nature.

In these finer pieces made by custom shops, one will find bevelled glass, designs created from stained glass, and extensive carving—in oak, mahogany or walnut. Although Empire can be seen as the base style for much factory-made golden oak, this is not nearly as prominent in the products of custom shops, whose overall look owes more to the incredible, fanciful, high-relief carving that could only be executed by hand. Hairy paw feet from Empire designs were certainly a mainstay of factory furniture, but the ferocious-animal motif was more fully embodied on custom pieces in the form of satyrs, dragons, griffins, and other mythical beasts.

---

6. Ibid., 34..

Fig. 7-4 A remarkable c. 1880 11-piece oak dining room suite (Figs. 7-4 through 7-7), consisting of six side chairs, two armchairs, dining table, sideboard, and server. The suite's provenance indicates that it was purchased directly from R. J. Horner in New York City in the 1880s. Horner's work often blurs the distinction between sculpture and furniture. Chairs (two pictured) with acanthus-carved stiles topped off by bust carving, crests with scrolling acanthus. Scrolling arms with flat acanthus carving. Plain seat rails with dropped scrolling decoration. Cabriole legs with knee carving and paw feet, joined by curving H-stretcher. On casters. *Courtesy Morton Goldberg Auction Gallery, New Orleans.* Set of eight chairs alone: **$3,600–4,800**.

Fig. 7-5 Oak server from the suite. Panelled gallery with cupid and cabochon crest. Gadrooned and shaped serving area over frieze carved with fantastic mythical beasts and gadrooned urn, flanked by high-relief masks. Supported by bearded-male forms entwined with rams and fruit and terminating in prominent human feet (an unusual touch). Panelled back and shaped, molded shelf over mask/paw feet. Server alone: **$1,500–2,500**.

Fig. 7-6 Oak dining table from the suite. Gadrooned edge over profusely carved frieze with Renaissance-type scrolls, vines, ribbons and masks. Supported by massive acanthus-carved pedestal and four winged-female figures with acanthus skirts and large paw feet. With several leaves to enlarge this grand table. Table alone: **$3,500–4,800**.

Fig. 7-7 Oak sideboard from the suite. The base uses motifs from the server, with the male/ram columns, paw/mask feet, gadrooned top edge, and projecting masks. Two cabinet doors with putti, masks, ribbons and Renaissance scrolls. Drawers similarly carved. Top with mirrored back flanked by mythical beast supporting complex crest of entwined scrolls, putti and satyrs centering cabochon and plumes. Sideboard alone: **$6,000–8,000**. The set: **$15,000–25,000**.

Pressed oak side chair, c. 1900, with elaborate well-turned spindle back and turned-spindle front stretchers, caned seat. Note also the twist-turning on uprights of the back and a scalloped front apron. Such points put the quality of these chairs far above the average. *Courtesy The Antique Emporium, Raleigh, N.C.* **$1,200–1,500** set of eight.

One of a pair of walnut pressed-back chairs, c. 1890, with pretty rococo-type pressed decoration and burl panels, spindles, turned front stretchers and legs. 41½″ high × 16½″ deep × 17½″ wide. Such chairs in walnut are extremely rare. *Courtesy Blair Hotel Antiques, Pittsboro, N.C.* **$350–475** the pair.

Oak sculpted-back dining chair from a set of twelve, c. 1890, with caned seat, turned spindles and legs, crest rail with carrying cutout. Refinished. 33″ high. *Private collection.* **$1,500–2,400** set of twelve.

Oak potty armchair, c. 1890, with pressed decoration, turned spindles. *Courtesy Depot Antiques, Hillsborough, N.C.* **$100–175**.

Left: Oak rocker with lion's-head arms, c. 1890. **$225–325**. Back: Flame oak and straight-grain oak lady's fall-front desk, c. 1890, with drawer raised on shaped legs. **$450–650**. Center: Oak library table, c. 1890, with spiral turning, paw feet. **$800–1,200**. Right: Lion-carved oak armchair, c. 1890. **$600–900**. *Courtesy Pettigrew Auction Gallery, Colorado Springs.*

Oak couch with back that folds down to create a bed, c. 1890. The late 19th century produced many versions of sofas that converted into beds. This would have been a relatively affordable model, and one probably available through mail order. *Courtesy Eileen Zambarda, 64 East Antiques, Asheboro, N.C.* **$600–900.**

Heavily carved oak dining table, c. 1890, with griffin base, carved frieze, pedestal and base for griffins. If not expandable with leaves, such tables were used in libraries. Attributed to R. J. Horner, New York City. Obviously a high-style example for an opulent era. *Courtesy Witherell Americana Auctions, Elk Grove, Calif.* Dealer estimate: **$2,500–3,500.**

Oak pedestal dining table, c. 1900, with four original leaves (not shown). Solid oak top over pedestal with four massive paw feet. The massive pedestal table is found in a multitude of variations. 54″ diameter. *Courtesy Southampton Antiques, Southampton, Mass.* **$900–1,500** as shown. Note that this table can become elaborate but can be simpler as well. Tables with *no* carved feet, only an Empire Revival scroll, were very common—especially via mail order—and sell for $450–750, depending on leaves, conditions, etc. Slightly more elaborate variations may have a lion's head at the top of the legs near the pedestal and sell for $1,200–1,800. Use this example as a benchmark to judge both more simple and more complex examples.

Carved mahogany partner's desk, c. 1890, with griffin base. Top with gadrooned edge over heavily scroll-carved frieze with three over two drawers. Attributed to R. J. Horner, New York City. *Courtesy Witherell Americana Auctions, Elk Grove, Calif.* Dealer estimate: **$6,000–8,000**.

Oak office furniture , c. 1900: Three-drawer file cabinet. **$450–650**. Bookcase with ten glass doors over four panelled drawers. **$1,200–1,800**. S-scroll rolltop desk of plain style with panelled sides. **$750–1,250**. Swivel desk chair. **$275–375**. *Courtesy Pettigrew Auction Gallery, Colorado Springs.*

Carved oak partner's desk, c. 1890. The four corners having relief-carved Jenny Lind–type busts of women, the panelled drawers with carved pulls. Acanthus-carved knees and paw feet. 55″ wide × 38″ deep × 30″ high. *Courtesy James D. Julia, Inc., Fairfield, Maine.* **$3,600–4,800**.

Another simple and widely found piece—the golden oak Larkin desk, c. 1890. With applied stylized acanthus carving on back and slant front. Interior with cubbyholes. 5′ high. *Courtesy Depot Antiques, Hillsborough, N.C.* **$500–700**.

Oak D-shaped china closet, c. 1895, with curved glass sides flanking central door. Resting on paw feet. Old, dark finish. 4½′ high. *Private collection.* **$650–950**.

Oak secretary of simple form, c. 1890. Incised decoration, raised-panel slant front with fitted interior, over four drawers with molded edges. 27″ wide × 16½″ deep × 5′2″ high. *Courtesy Blair Hotel Antiques, Pittsboro, N.C.* **$800–1,200**.

Oak china closet with curved glass sides, c. 1890. Central serpentine door. Columns headed by lions. Paw feet. Scroll-carved cornice. *Courtesy Pettigrew Auction Gallery, Colorado Springs.* **$2,000–4,000**.

Ebonized Empire Revival bookcase, c. 1890, with bevelled glass door flanked by columns ending in paw feet and topped with corinthian capitals. Break-fronted cornice. Replaced plywood back. 40″ wide × 64″ high. *Courtesy Eileen Zambarda, 64 East Antiques, Asheboro, N.C.* **$1,200–1,800**.

Mahogany side cabinet, c. 1890. Base resting on six paw feet. Two bevelled-glass doors centering two smaller doors over central open recessed area. Top with mirrored back and attenuated columns supporting two pagoda-like "roofs," centering open area for display with upper shelf and fret-carved gallery. With lots of delicate applied carving and fret carving, there is a fineness to the detail that makes this piece different from the massive oak pieces also popular at the time. This model retains its original "diamond dust" mirrors and cast-iron latticework details at the juncture of the feet and base. In original, mint condition. *Courtesy 19th Century America, Lafayette, La.* Dealer estimate: **$5,000–7,500**.

Oak sideboard, c. 1890, with mirrored backsplash topped by fabulous mythical beasts with scrolling manes. Marble surface above three over two drawers over two cabinet doors with Renaissance-inspired carving, divided by fluted pilasters. Panelled sides. 54″ long × 23″ deep × 5′5″ high. *Courtesy L & L Antiques, Hickory, N.C.* **$1,800–2,600**.

Opulent-period mahogany sideboard by R. J. Horner, New York City, c. 1880–1900. Much of his work shows this profuse Renaissance-inspired carving including mythical beasts, like the "dolphins" on the canted corners. Base on scroll feet with four cabinet doors and one drawer below three frieze drawers, all profusely carved. Serving area backed by large bevelled mirror. Carved columns support the massive scrolling pediment. Also with two display shelves. *Courtesy Southampton Antiques, Southampton, Mass.* **$8,000–12,000.**

Oak hallstand, c. 1890, with hooks, bevelled mirror, seat with lift lid for storage. Typical simple 1890s form that was standard issue from catalog firms. With applied scrolling acanthus and rolling pin–type decoration. 74″ high. *Courtesy Blair Hotel Antiques, Pittsboro, N.C.* **$900–1,200.**

Opulent oak hall bench, c. 1890, absolutely encrusted with carving. Arms supported by winged lions. Seat lifts for storage. Base with scrolling foliage and mask carving. Paw feet. 65″ wide × 47″ high. *Courtesy Pettigrew Auction Gallery, Colorado Springs.* **$3,000–4,800.**

189

Golden oak bedroom suite, c. 1890. In general, golden oak furniture uses modified heavy Empire forms and employs figured oak veneer in the same way flame mahogany veneer was used on Empire furniture—the wood grain itself supplies the decorative interest. This type of cornice is limited to golden oak furniture—with cigarlike bar surmounted by scrolls. *Courtesy Morton Goldberg Auction Gallery, New Orleans*. Dresser: **$900–1,500**. Washstand: **$475–675**.

Golden oak dresser, c. 1890, with applied acanthus and scroll carving. Oak and oak veneer. Slightly bowed drawers. Bevelled mirror. 40″ wide × 76″ high. *Courtesy Calico Quilt, Goldston, N.C.* **$300–500**.

Wardrobe from the suite. Base with configuration similar to dressers, with stepped-back upper section. Two mirrored doors, upper edges framed in scrolling acanthus, flanked by columns and divided by panel with applied carving. Cornice similar to those on dressers. Panelled sides. *Courtesy Morton Goldberg Auction Gallery, New Orleans*. **$1,500–2,400**.

Mail-order-type tall chests with mirrors, c. 1900–1920. Left: With serpentine-fronted drawers. Mahoganized maple or cherry. **$400–600**. Middle: Oak with applied scrolled carving on drawer faces. **$375–575**. Right: Narrow chest with panelled sides. Original finish. **$275–375**. These forms take us to the end of the Victorian period; we are now moving into the era dominated by factory-produced Colonial Revival furniture, represented in this photo by the chair (for extensive reference, see our book *Colonial Revival Furniture with Prices*). *Courtesy Pettigrew Auction Gallery, Colorado Springs.*

Panelled bedstead from the suite. Footboard with applied acanthus carving and rolling pin–type crest. Headboard similarly decorated. The table is Eastlake and was not part of the original suite. *Courtesy Morton Goldberg Auction Gallery, New Orleans.* **$900–1,500**.

BIBLIOGRAPHY

Ames, Kenneth L., ed. *Victorian Furniture: Essays from a Victorian Society Autumn Symposium.* Philadelphia: Victorian Society in America, 1983. Published as *Nineteenth Century* 8, nos. 3–4 (1982).

———. *Death in the Dining Room and Other Tales of Victorian Culture.* Philadelphia: Temple University Press, 1992.

———. "Designed in France: Notes on the Transmission of French Styles to America." *Winterthur Portfolio* 12 (1977): 103–14.

———. "Grand Rapids Furniture at the Time of the Centennial." *Winterthur Portfolio* 10 (1975): 23–50.

———. "The Rocking Chair in 19th Century America." *The Magazine Antiques* 103 (1973): 322–327.

———. "Sitting in (Néo-Grec) Style." *Nineteenth Century* 2, nos. 3–4 (Autumn 1976): 50–58.

———. "What is the Néo-Grec?" *Nineteenth Century* 2, no. 2 (Summer 1976): 12–21.

Art and Antiques, ed. *Nineteenth Century Furniture: Innovation, Revival and Reform.* Introduction by Mary Jean Madigan. New York: Billboard Publications, an Art and Antiques Book, 1982.

Aslin, Elizabeth. *The Aesthetic Movement: Prelude to Art Nouveau.* New York: A. Praeger, 1969.

Bates, Elizabeth Bidwell and Jonathan L. Fairbanks. *American Furniture, 1620 to the Present.* New York: Richard Marek Publishers, 1981.

Bishop, Robert and Patricia Coblentz. *The World of Antiques, Art, and Architecture in Victorian America.* New York: E. P. Dutton, 1979.

Blundell, Peter S. *Market Place Guide to Oak Furniture—Styles and Values.* Paducah, Ky.: Collector Books, 1980.

Burke, Doreen Bolger, et al. *In Pursuit of Beauty: Americans and the Aesthetic Movement.* New York: Rizzoli International Publications in association with the Metropolitan Museum of Art, 1986.

Butler, Joseph T. *American Antiques 1800–1900.* New York: The Odyssey Press, 1969.

Cook, Clarence. *The House Beautiful: Essays on Beds, Tables, Stools, and Candlesticks.* New York: Scribner, Armstrong and Company, 1878. Reprint, Croton-on-Hudson, N.Y.: North River Press, 1980.

Darling, Sharon. *Chicago Furniture: Art, Craft and Industry, 1833–1983.* New York: W. W. Norton, 1984.

Dietz, Ulysses G. *Century of Revivals: 19th-Century American Furniture from the Collection of the Newark Museum.* Newark, N.J.: Newark Museum of Art, 1983.

Downing, Andrew Jackson. *The Architecture of Country Houses Including Designs for Cottages, and Farm-Houses, and Villas, with Remarks on Interiors, Furniture, and the Best Modes of*

Warming and Ventilating. New York: D. Appleton, 1850; reprint, New York: Dover Publications, 1969.

Dubrow, Eileen and Richard. *American Furniture of the Nineteenth Century, 1840–1880.* Exton, Penna: Schiffer Publishing, Ltd., 1983.

———. *Made in America 1875–1905.* West Chester, Penna.: Schiffer Publishing, Ltd., 1982.

Eastlake, Charles. *Hints on Household Taste in Furniture, Upholstery, and Other Details.* London: Longmans, Green & Co., 1868. 2nd edition 1869. 3rd edition 1872. 4th revised edition 1878 (this edition reprinted by Dover Publications, New York, 1969). In America, 1st edition 1872, 2nd edition 1874. 3rd edition 1875. 4th edition 1876. 5th edition 1877.

Ettema, Michael J. "Technological Innovation and Design Economics in Furniture Manufacture." *Winterthur Portfolio* 16, nos. 2/3 (Summer/Autumn 1981): 197–233.

Fitzgerald, Oscar P. *Three Centuries of American Furniture.* Englewood Cliffs, N.J.: Prentice-Hall, 1982.

Garrett, Wendell. *Victorian America: Classical Romanticism to Guilded Opulence.* New York: Rizzoli International Publications, 1993.

Gloag, John. *Victorian Comfort: A Social History of Design from 1830–1900.* New York: Macmillan Company, 1961.

Grier, Katherine. *Culture and Comfort: People, Parlors, and Upholstery, 1850–1930.* Amherst: University of Massachusetts Press, 1988.

Grover, Kathryn, ed. *Dining in America, 1850–1900.* Amherst: University of Massachusetts Press, 1987.

Hanks, David. *Innovative Furniture in America 1800 to the Present.* New York: Horizon Press, 1981.

Hauserman, Diane D. "Alexander Roux and His 'Plain and Artistic Furniture'."

The Magazine Antiques 93, no. 2 (February 1968): 210–217.

Hosley, William. *The Japan Idea: Art and Life in Victorian America.* Hartford, Conn.: Wadsworth Atheneum, 1990.

Howe, D. W., ed. *Victorian America.* Philadelphia: University of Pennsylvania Press, 1976.

Howe, Katherine S. and David B. Warren. *The Gothic Revival Style in America, 1830–1870.* Houston: Museum of Fine Arts, 1976.

Howe, Katherine S., Alice Cooney Frelinghuysen and Catherine Hoover Voorsanger. *Herter Brothers: Furniture and Interiors for a Gilded Age.* New York: Harry N. Abrams, Inc., 1994.

Johnson, J. Stewart. "John Jelliff, Cabinetmaker." *The Magazine Antiques* 206 (August 1972): 256–260.

MacKay, James. *Turn of the Century Antiques.* New York: Dutton, 1974.

Madigan, Mary Jean Smith. *Eastlake-Influenced American Furniture 1870–1890.* Yonkers, N.Y.: Hudson River Museum, 1973.

———. "The Influence of Charles Locke Eastlake on American Furniture Manufacture, 1870–90." *Winterthur Portfolio* 10 (1975): 1–22.

McClaugherty, Martha Crabill. "Household Art: Creating the Artistic Home, 1868–1893." *Winterthur Portfolio* 18, no. 1 (Spring 1983): 1–26.

Meeks, Carroll L. V. *The Railroad Station.* New Haven: Yale University Press, 1956.

Nineteenth-Century America: Furniture and Other Decorative Arts. Introduction by Berry B. Tracy. New York: Metropolitan Museum of Art, 1970.

Ormsbee, Thomas H. *Field Guide to American Victorian Furniture.* Boston and Toronto: Little, Brown and Company, 1952.

Otto, Cecelia Jackson. *American Furniture of the Nineteenth Century.* New York: The Viking Press, 1965.

———. "Pillar and Scroll: Greek Revival Furniture of the 1830s." *The Magazine Antiques* 81 (May 1962): 504–507.

Pearce, John N. and Lorraine W. Pearce. "More on the Meeks Cabinetmakers." *The Magazine Antiques* 90 (July 1966): 69–73.

Pearce, John N., Lorraine W. Pearce, and Robert C. Smith. "The Meeks Family of Cabinetmakers." *The Magazine Antiques* 85 (April 1964): 414–420.

Peirce, Donald C. "Mitchell and Rammelsberg: Cincinnati Furniture Manufacturers, 1847–1881." *Winterthur Portfolio* 13 (1979): 209–29.

Ransom, Frank Edward. *The City Built on Wood: The History of the Furniture Industry in Grand Rapids, Michigan 1850–1950.* Ann Arbor, Mich.: Edwards Brothers, 1955.

Schwartz, Marvin D., Edward J. Stanek, and Douglas K. True. *The Furniture of John Henry Belter and the Rococo Revival: An Inquiry into Nineteenth-Century Furniture Design through a Study of the Gloria and Richard Manney Collection.* New York: E. P. Dutton, 1981.

Smith, Robert C. "Gothic and Elizabethan Revival Furniture, 1800–1850." *The Magazine Antiques* 75 (March 1959): 272–276.

Spofford, Harriet. *Art Decoration Applied to Furniture.* New York: Harper and Brothers, 1878.

Stevenson, Louise. *The Victorian Homefront: American Thought and Culture, 1860–1880.* Boston: Twayne, 1991.

Strickland, Peter L. L. "Furniture by the Lejambre Family of Philadelphia." *The Magazine Antiques* 113, no. 3 (March 1978): 600–613.

Walters, Betty Lawson. "The King of Desks: Wooton's Patent Secretary." *Smithsonian Studies in History and Technology* No. 3 (1969): 1–22.

Weidman, Gregory R. *Furniture in Maryland, 1740–1940.* Baltimore: Maryland Historical Society, 1984.

Winkler, Gail and Roger W. Moss. *Victorian Interior Decoration: American Interiors 1830–1900.* New York: Holt, 1986.

CONTRIBUTORS

The Antique Mall, Inc.
387 Ja-Max Drive
Hillsborough, NC 27278
(919) 732-8882

Antiques Emporium
Cameron Village
2060 Clark Avenue
Raleigh, NC 27605
(919) 834-7250

Blair Hotel Antiques
11 Hillsboro Street
Pittsboro, NC 27312
(919) 542-1141

Joan Bogart
Box 265
Rockville Centre, NY 11571
(516) 764-5286

Frank H. Boos Auction Gallery
420 Enterprise Court
Bloomfield Hills, MI 48301
(810) 332-1500

Butterfield & Butterfield
7601 Sunset Boulevard
Los Angeles, CA 90046
(213) 850-7500

The Butterfly—Fine Antiques
Willow Lane Shop
4422 Chapel Hill Boulevard
Durham, NC 27707

Butte's Antiques
127 Williamsboro Street
Oxford, NC 27565
(919) 693-6278

Byrum Furniture and Antiques
117 Morris Street
Hertford, NC 27944
(919) 426-7478

Calico Quilt
PO Box 249
Goldston, NC 27252
(919) 898-4998

Carolina Antique Mall
Cameron Village
2060 Clark Avenue
Raleigh, NC 27605
(919) 833-8227

Crabtree & Company Antiques
Carthage Street
Cameron, NC
(910) 245-3163

Depot Antiques
Daniel Boone Village
Hillsborough, NC 27278
(919) 732-9796

Edwards Antiques and Collectibles
302 Hillsboro Street
Pittsboro, NC 27312
(919) 542-5649

Flomaton Antique Auction
207 Palafox Street
Flomaton, AL 36441
(334) 296-3059

Frederick Craddock III Antiques
Lynchburg, VA

The Flying Eagle Galleries
4422 Durham Chapel Hill Boulevard
Durham, NC 27707
(919) 489-3653

Freeman\Fine Arts
1808-10 Chestnut Street
Philadelphia, PA 19103
(215) 563-9275

Morton Goldberg Auction Galleries
547 Baronne Street
New Orleans, LA 70113
(504) 592-2300

Grogan & Company
890 Commonwealth Ave.
Boston, MA 02215
(617) 566-4100

Heritage House Antiques
PO Box 245
Bland, VA 24315
(703) 688-3755

Leslie Hindman Auctioneers
215 West Ohio Street
Chicago, IL 60610
(312) 670-0010

James D. Julia, Inc.
PO Box 830
Fairfield, ME 04937
(207) 453-7125

L & L Antiques
4025 Hwy. 70 S.W.
Hickory, NC 28601
(704) 328-9373

Merrywood Antiques
5608 Patterson Ave.
Richmond, VA 23226
(804) 288-9309

Neal Auction Company
4038 Magazine Street
New Orleans, LA 70115
(504) 899-5329

New Orleans Auction Gallery, Inc.
801 Magazine Street
New Orleans, LA 70130
(504) 566-1849

19th Century America
3603 Johnston Street
Lafayette, LA 70501
(318) 988-1020

Pettigrew Auction Gallery
1645 South Tejon Street
Colorado Springs, CO 80906
(719) 633-7963

Rudy's Antiques
3324 Virginia Beach Boulevard
Virginia Beach, VA 23452
(804) 340-2079

64 East Antiques and Collectibles
4660 U.S. Hwy. 64 East
Franklinville, NC 27248
(910) 824-1542

Skinner, Inc.
Auctioneers and Appraisers of Fine Art
63 Park Plaza
Boston, MA 02116
(617) 350-5400

Kimball M. Sterling
125 W. Market Street
Johnson City, TN 37601
(615) 928-1471

Southampton Antiques
172 College Highway (Route 10)
Southampton, MA 01073
(413) 527-1022

Turner Antiques, Ltd.
Madison Avenue Antiques Center #6
760 Madison Avenue
New York, NY 10021

Whitehall at the Villa
1213 East Franklin Street
Chapel Hill, NC 27514
(919) 942-3179

Witherell Americana Auctions
3620 West Island Court
Elk Grove, CA 95758
(916) 683-3266

Woodbine Antiques
213 College Street
Oxford, NC 27565
(919) 693-2973

INDEX